little "d"
deacon

little "d" deacon

servants without a title

Jerald McGowin

For speaker scheduling: luplifts@gmail.com

ARPress
ILLUMINATING IDEAS,
EMPOWERING VOICES

ARPress
45 Dan Road Suite 5
Canton MA 02021

Hotline: 1(800) 220-7660
Fax: 1(855) 752-6001

Ordering Information:
Quantity sales. Special discounts are available on quantity purchases by corporations, associations, and others. For details, contact the publisher at the address above.

Printed in the United States of America.

ISBN-13:   Softcover   979-8-89356-690-1
                   eBook   979-8-89356-691-8

Library of Congress Control Number: 2024904630

CONTENTS

DEDICATION

May the Lord's Church be blessed by this little book.

To My Beloved,
Who loves me greatly!

To my Father
Who taught me the value of:
Duty

To my many Mentors
Brother Knox, Brother Thomas, who are with Jesus,
The greatest prayer warriors and evangelists
I have ever known.
Brother Hagood:
Who taught me to Love the Church even when
the Church does not love their Pastor.
Brother Herb Thomas:
Who taught me that healing from a Church wound does come.
Brother Holcomb:
Who taught me more about the Bible than any Samford or
NOBTS Class.
Brothers Roy and James, who are now with Jesus:
My first two deacons who loved me unconditionally.
To my Pastor buddies: Brad, Joseph, Rob,
Bill, Herb, and many others.
To Brother Al, who knows how to encourage.
To Brother Steve
A new Baptist and a little "d" deacon who gave
me the idea for this little book title.

May God be glorified in this endeavor:
May little "d" deacons, ever spark a great revival by their ministries.

PREFACE

T he title to this little book may be surprising to many! For most active Church going folks, we normally associate the word **deacon** to a well-respected, beloved individual. We usually would associate the word **deacon** to a title. Over many years since the formation of deacons in the Book of Acts the word **deacon** stopped being a descriptor of the job of deacon and increasingly became a title, much like aristocratic England with barons, knights, lords, and dukes. This is an intentional analogy. This was not the case in the early Church. Sadly, many deacons have become titled men rather than servant men. This little book is a simplified call for God's deacons to rise up and discard the title of **Deacon** and return to the Biblical mandate for deacons, and by their good works establish a framework for God's Revival Fire.

Big "D" deacons are titled men who often enjoy being called Deacon Jones and are usually only nominally engaged in ministry. Too many times they have inherited their positions or are one of the last eligible males in their congregation. They have been ordained and refer to themselves as Deacon Jones. They meet monthly and generally discuss anything but ministry, usually focusing on financial matters or the state of the Church and often find themselves in a situation where they actively engage in undermining the Pastor or worse. They are happy with the status quo and are often the source of opposition to even the most minor changes. Likely they sit on key committees and perform many administrative tasks. Sometimes they even consider themselves as the Supervisory Committee to oversee the Pastor. When this happens, that local Church ceases to be a Bible Based Church. **THIS BOOK IS NOT FOR BIG "D" Deacons.** This book is for those who are actively seeking the underlying Biblical principle for little **"d" deacon ministry**. Little "d" deacon ministry will be a new term and hopefully a call for a renewed interest in little "d" deacon Bible rooted ministry.

Big "D" Deacons are the kind of Deacons most people are familiar with. Fortunately, Big "D" Deacons are not found in Scripture and **every** Big "D" Deacon operates contrary to Scripture. **THIS BOOK** is for deacons, Pastors and Churches who have a high view of Scripture and desire to fulfill the role of deacon well.

The most basic understanding of the word "DEACON" is servant, and not a paid servant, either. **A little "d" deacon is one who is consumed in their desire to serve God's people,** not for personal gain, but solely for the purpose of Glorifying God.

We live in a day of declining morals; declining nations; declining families; declining ethics and declining churches. From a Christian perspective we live in a declining world. Church members are growing older and fewer young people are interested in continuing in a local church that has no history or purpose for them. Families who once existed for generations in one local church is almost entirely forgotten and fading into myth and legend. The question arises what is to be done? Is it hopeless? Is all lost? The answer lies where it has always been! **The answer is in the great Living Word of God!**

The scope of this little book is confined to deacons and to a lesser degree Pastors and their ministries; however, it is of the utmost importance to the local Church. **We must return to the Gospel and make our mark in history as Churches of every age have done.** We must remember we are a called people to **THIS** generation. We must not cry about the last generation any longer, but turn our focus to this present age and telling the GOOD NEWS to this desperate generation. **Let us not allow our local Church to become a Laodicean Church!** We may live in the Laodicean Age, but we do not have to be a member of that Church. The only answer for all ages and every generation is **Jesus Christ, the only Messiah** of all Creation. As a Church, allow Jesus to be Jesus, turning loose the Holy Spirit to be a consuming fire in our Churches, and let God the Father, be God! We must set God free from the box we have tried to put Him in. This requires us to become more Biblically focused as a Church and more evangelistic to a desperate world. As we approach the latter days, little "d" deacon ministry is going to take on an ever increasingly important role. Intentional Ministry is evangelism. A food pantry and clothing closet are good things for the world to be doing. But if the Church wishes to meet this need, let every contact be filled with the Gospel.

Perhaps you recall hearing pastors calling the Church to become more like the first century Church. Seldom does this generation hear this call. We live in a world that is becoming more and more like the world of the first century Church and less and less like the Church of the First Century. In practical terms this means the World is becoming more spiritually desperate and the Church less Spiritually Active. Christian businesspeople are being targeted solely to drive them from business and destroy their livelihoods. This was occurring under the Roman Empire during the first century. We also see this happening to the Coptic[1] Church (Egyptian Christian Church) in Egypt. The Apostle John, in his vivid account in Revelation presents worldwide persecution as the **<u>norm</u>** of **John's Day and in the last days**. Churches around the world are being targeted with violence and fire. Ancient Churches in Iraq and Syria are being razed to the ground. In Africa children of believers are being taken from their families to rape, to kill and to be sold into bondage. In the United States racism is used as a political weapon in the most incendiary way. The Democratic Party routinely uses these tactics to further their political ambitions. While the Republican Party, when they are in power, fail to live up to their promises as well. Political Parties are not the answer. The Government is not the answer. Only Jesus Christ is the answer. The Government and the Political parties are the problem.

Persecution is real. It is our modern reality. Most of the World suffers from persecution. In Africa and the Middle East, **SLAVERY IS REAL, and the Saints of God are being targeted for destruction.**

---

[1] an Afro-Asiatic language descended from ancient Egyptian and used as the liturgical language of the Coptic church. https://www.merriam-webster.com/dictionary/Coptic

Even in the United States some are being used as sex slaves. Slavery is real in our modern age. This recalls a comment of Jesus:

> NKJV John 10:10 The thief cometh not, but for to steal, and to kill, and to destroy: I am come that they might have life, and that they might have *it* more abundantly.[2]

The believer, in most of the World, is in imminent danger. Churches on every continent have suffered persecution. Saints of God are being added daily to the kingdom of God by the swords of radical Islam. Persecution is coming for every Church that preaches the Good News of Jesus Christ. Clearly the world is as a thief in the night and our only hope is Jesus. This is an old story; Jesus faced it and we **WILL** face it too.

We must not lose sight that there still is **JOY** in the World; **HOPE** is found here as well, and there is still **PEACE in Jesus**. The World cannot destroy these things though it tries. Jesus came to give us **ABUNDANT LIFE** not an "ok" life. We can have **more HOPE, more JOY,** and **more PEACE**. Our Church can still be on Fire for Jesus.

Prior to **World War II, the Jews were not the only ones targeted** by the Nazis. Gypsies[3] and some Christians were later targeted. Dietrich Bonhoeffer is the most widely known Christian who was martyred during this horrible time. It seems likely that the coming persecution will mirror the Nazi-German approach to persecute Christian Churches. Likely persecution will come under a different banner than what Nazis used, but it will almost certainly use similar tactics to attack the people of God. Churches **who do not stand** in opposition to the anti-Christ likely will not suffer. The Churches of God need to prepare for the imminent battle that is sure to come to the front porch of every faithful

---

[2] *The Holy Bible: King James Version*, Electronic Edition of the 1900 Authorized Version. (Bellingham, WA: Logos Research Systems, Inc., 2009), Jn 10:10.

[3] gyp·sya ['jipsē]: **noun English Language Learners Definition of *Gypsy*:** : a member of a group of people who originally came from northern India and now live mostly in Asia, Europe, and North America. https://www.merriam-webster.com/dictionary/gypsy

Church. The Apostle John must have considered that all the persecution in his day was leading to the last days, while he recorded what was revealed to him by Jesus Christ. We see in the Apostle John's writings that Jesus called the Church to endure until the end. We are called to do likewise – proclaiming the Gospel to the last breath. Let us make our mark on this generation for Christ Jesus' Kingdom. Is it possible that what is happening to Christians in the Middle East, Asia and Africa will one day come to the United States? It is already on our doorstep! How long until it is on the front porch of every faithful Church of God? The only option is to return to the Gospel of Jesus Christ and relearn the lessons of the First Century Church. If we are called to be persecuted let us endure and be found faithful to the Lord of lords and the King of kings. Let us endure to the end: proclaiming and glorifying God even to our last breath!

The last Book of the Bible is concerned with the last 7 years of Human History. Many Evangelicals believe that we are fast approaching the days before the Great Tribulation. Indeed, it seems likely that the Apostle John, the human recorder of Revelation, believed the last days were at hand. Down through the ages people have thought/believed the Last Days were upon them. And today's Church is no different, nor should it be. The Church was called into existence to be "Fishers of Men". This call is still in effect. It has never been recalled and will be an enduring call to the Church until Jesus comes.

Many cults have wasted their lives in preparation for the Last Days: some committed mass suicide; others have fallen into distant memory. The point is quite simple, our concern should not – must not - be consumed with the Prophecy of the Last Days. We are called to be Christians in whatever age we are found. Jesus has spoken to the ages that HIS people are called to overcome this world. Overcoming may mean many things, but one thing is certain: we are to remain faithful to the call Jesus Christ has placed upon us. We have Jesus' promises. One example is as follows:

NKJV Revelation 2: 26 And he who overcomes, and keeps My works until the end, to him I will give power over the nations—[27]'He shall rule them with a rod of iron; They shall be dashed to pieces like the potter's vessels'—as I also have received from My Father; [28] and I will give him the morning star.

[29] "He who has an ear, let him hear what the Spirit says to the churches.'"

The following is an alternate translation of the same passage:

I will let those people who are victorious (who conquer), who continue to obey my commands until the end of time (or, the world), have the same power to rule that my Father has given to me: I will let them have the authority to rule over all the nations (or, tribes). They will rule over them without mercy and will shatter them into pieces just like people break pots made from clay. I will also give them the morning star to show (or, demonstrate) their victory.[4]

It should be our heart's desire that little "d" deacons and prospective deacons consider returning to the model of the First Century Church and thereby spark a great revival in our local Churches. This will not be easy, for there will be big "D" deacons who will stand in the way. Believing and embracing the role of little "d" deacons, the embers of revival will begin to glow, and from this a mighty Revival Fire might spring forth. The Book of Acts tells of one such revival sparked by little "d" deacons and it is our prayer that our Churches will experience a revival fire similar to the ones experienced at the Jerusalem Church when **deacon ministry ignited an early REVIVAL FIRE.**

Sean Hannity and Glenn Beck, both conservative radio personalities, and to a lesser degree Rush Limbaugh have highlighted Christian persecution both in the United States and abroad. Each of these men

---

[4]   Robert G. Bratcher and H. Hatton, *A Handbook on the Revelation to John*, UBS Handbook Series (New York: United Bible Societies, 1993), 65.

have rightly noticed the decline of Western Values, particularly values common to the United States citizenry, such as Freedom and Liberty. Thankfully, men like these have highlighted Christian persecution and raised the question: Why does the US fail to allow these Christians to enter the US based on asylum? Senator Shelby of Alabama and Congressman Aderholt (also from Alabama) have not answered this question! It seems logical to allow Christians under persecution to immigrate as they would be much more likely to embrace the historic American dream. Let us pray that more well-known figures will embrace this need.

In Acts chapter 6, deacons come on the scene and the Church explodes in growth. The reason is simple, people outside saw that the Church was ministering to people in need. **The purpose of this little book is to inspire Pastors and Churches to free their deacons from administrative tasks and to focus on ministry and use the deacons of the First Century Church as the model for deacon ministry.**

CHAPTER ONE

Servant – Service – Servanthood

Tracing the doctrine of Servanthood from Ancient Israel to modern deacons.

Servant, service, and servanthood are not generally considered noble words. For most people these are words that are demeaning and harken back to the days of slavery or some other form of menial work. The Roman Empire operated on a slave - based economic system (as did the old South); in this system servants were menials. Slavery usually meant that a group of people were displaced and sold as commodities, such as: field slaves, household slaves, instructors, and as entertainment (gladiators). Roman conquests generated many slaves. Though not all went to Rome, they were generally displaced. It was and is a horrible system commonly found during the times of Jesus' ministry.

During the time prior to the American Civil War, and in our present age where sex slaves are a new commodity sold to whoever is willing to pay the price, slavery is still a horrible institution (Glenn Beck, in the secular world is funding some activities to free people caught in the sex trade). In Ancient Israel slavery of Jews to Jews was mainly a form of indentured servitude that could last no more than fifty years. One entered slavery as a last resort. Unfortunately for ancient Israel, they failed to keep the years of Jubilee[5]. No evidence has been found to date

---

[5] **Notes for: Leviticus 25:10**
 tn *Heb* "the year of the fifty years," or perhaps "the year, fifty years" (GKC 435 §134.*o*, note 2).
 tn Cf. KJV, ASV, NAB, NIV, NRSV "liberty"; TEV, CEV "freedom." The characteristics of this "release" are detailed in the following verses. For

to show that Israel followed the commandment to honor the Jubilee years. It is thought that because of these failures the nation of Israel suffered judgments of God for their failure to treat the most desperate of God's people fairly. Certainly, seven years is a long time to suffer slavery. Presumably, the clear majority did not enter slavery year one but entered due to some extraordinary action; either by war, famine, or other societal failure. Sometimes these persons entered voluntary permanent servitude.

> **NKJV Leviticus 25:10 And you shall consecrate the fiftieth year and proclaim liberty throughout *all* the land to all its inhabitants. It shall be a Jubilee for you; and each of you shall return to his possession, and each of you shall return to his family.**
>
> **¹¹That fiftieth year shall be a Jubilee to you; in it you shall neither sow nor reap what grows of its own accord, nor gather *the grapes* of your untended vine.**
>
> **¹²For it *is* the Jubilee; it shall be holy to you; you shall eat its produce from the field.**
>
> **¹³'In this Year of Jubilee, each of you shall return to his possession.**

---

substantial summaries and bibliography on the biblical and ancient Near Eastern material regarding such a "release" see J. E. Hartley, *Leviticus* (WBC), 427–34, and B. A. Levine, *Leviticus* (JPSTC), 270–74.

tn *Heb* "A jubilee that shall be to you." Although there has been some significant debate about the original meaning of the Hebrew word translated "jubilee" (יוֹבֵל, *yovel*; see the summary in J. E. Hartley, *Leviticus* [WBC], 434), the term most likely means "ram" and can refer also to a "ram's horn." The fiftieth year would, therefore, be called the "jubilee" because of the associated sounding of the "ram's horn" (see B. A. Levine, *Leviticus* [JPSTC], 172, and the literature cited there). The Net Bible and the Net Bible notes from Logos Software.

Leviticus 25: 10 tells us about the 50-year Jubilee. It follows seven (7) Jubilees and here all property is returned to its rightful family, protecting the poorest of people and ensuring that the nation's wealth is not concentrated in the hands of the few. Every 50 years there would be a re-balancing of the national wealth. For more information about the price Israel paid for failing to honor the Jubilee system read the book of Nehemiah.

The Jubilee policy was far superior to any other ancient system concerning slavery and debt. Judging by other nations contemporary to ancient Israel, this was a system that provided every generation with a new start filled with hope and promise. Even though slavery is and was a horrible institution, God provided for His people a way of escape. Surely this must point to the day of redemption that God has promised to generations. Jesus is our redemption and the fulfillment of all the Old Testament! Jesus provided a way to escape the judgement of sin. Every seven years all of Israel should have been reminded of how God provides for his people. Freed slaves would have and should have been a reminder of God's mercy. The celebration of Jubilee points to the full and complete restoration of Israel. In the fiftieth year, slaves, debt and property were redeemed by God. In the seventh year of Jubilee, slaves and debt were redeemed. Forgiveness of debt and freedom was not the whole story.

> NKJV Deuteronomy 15:12 **"If your brother, a Hebrew man, or a Hebrew woman, is sold to you and serves you six years, then in the seventh year you shall let him go free from you.**
>
> **¹³And when you send him away free from you, you shall not let him go away empty-handed; ¹⁴ you shall supply him liberally from your flock, from your threshing floor, and from your winepress. *From what* the Lord has blessed you with, you shall give to him. ¹⁵ You shall remember that you were a slave in the land of Egypt, and the Lord your God redeemed you; therefore I command you this thing today.**

Every seven years Israel was to see a living tapestry of God's redemptive grace play out in Israel. All of Israel was to recall God's redemptive action in Egypt. God's protection, God's provision in the wilderness and God's fulfillment of HIS promise to Abraham. When God redeemed Israel, HE did not send them away empty handed from Egypt! When Israel freed the slaves:

> NKJV Exodus 3:21**And I will give this people favor in the sight of the Egyptians; and it shall be, when you go, that you shall not go empty-handed. ²² But every woman shall ask of her neighbor, namely, of her who dwells near her house, articles of silver, articles of gold, and clothing; and you shall put *them* on your sons and on your daughters. So you shall plunder the Egyptians."**

Slavery under Egyptian rule, during the days of Moses, was about as horrific as slavery could get. Yet even then, like the seventh year of Jubilee slaves were freed but not penniless. God provided! They were paid. And left slavery with the resources to never return to slavery. From God's point of view slavery (slavery in Israel) is not menial or demeaning. It is a means of social welfare. It had its purpose and place. Though Jesus was not referencing the laws of Jewish slavery HE did have some interesting things to say about slavery. For instance:

> NKJV Matthew 20:27**And whoever desires to be first among you, let him be your slave—²⁸ just as the Son of Man did not come to be served, but to serve, and to give His life as a ransom for many".**

These are the words of Jesus. Notice how Jesus took a horrific system and turned it upside down and used it as a teaching lesson. "All the world over, and all the ages, the ordinary man has seen dignity in **"being served"** and has seen a kind of indignity in "serving".[6] This has continued down to our day as well. It is better to be served than to do

---

[6]   H. D. M. Spence-Jones, ed., *St. Matthew*, vol. 2, The Pulpit Commentary (London; New York: Funk & Wagnalls Company, 1909), 311.

the serving. Jesus turned this upside down and measured greatness by serving others. It is the one doing the serving that is great! **This is a key concept for little "d" deacons!**

It is fair to ask: how did the served become more valued that the server!? Two possibilities have been suggested!

1. **Through the exaggerated importance given to *self*.** A man has come to be of more interest to himself than his brother can ever be to him. Yet God made man male and female in order to prevent this egoism, and start man upon working the altruistic principle, each finding his or her own best blessing in caring for the other. Christianity is the recovery of the primary altruistic principle, and the mastery of that egoism which has proved the prolific parent of all the vices.

2. **Through the absorbing interest of appearances; of material things**—state, wealth, luxury, show of greatness. True greatness lies in character; let us once see this clearly and receive it fully, and then the kindliness and thoughtfulness which sweetly blend with humility, and ever make us ready to serve, will seem to be surpassingly valuable.[7]

Materialism and ego are the enemies of any altruistic principle, including Christianity. It is those that serve people that are greatly esteemed before God. Serving people points others to Jesus. This is a basic tenet of the Salvation Army. Serving others matters and it should be a key tenet in all faith groups, not just the Salvation Army. The theme of service is a theme Jesus uses several times: both implied and explicitly, as in Matthew 20:

> [25]**But Jesus called them to *Himself* and said, "You know that the rulers of the Gentiles lord it over them, and those who are great exercise authority over them.**

---

[7]   H. D. M. Spence-Jones, ed., _St. Matthew_, vol. 2, The Pulpit Commentary (London; New York: Funk & Wagnalls Company, 1909), 311.

²⁶Yet it shall not be so among you; but whoever desires to become great among you, let him be your servant.
²⁷And whoever desires to be first among you, let him be your slave—
²⁸just as the Son of Man did not come to be served, but to serve, and to give His life as a ransom for many."[8]

and implicitly in other passages, such as the Lord's Supper; washing the disciples' feet; healing; feeding the multitudes and ultimately in Jesus' death, burial, and resurrection.

There is an important context to be considered surrounding Matthew 20: 27-28!

> The **great** and the **first** recall Jesus' previous teachings in 18:2–4; 19:30–20:16. Jesus had compared the humility of a true follower to that of a child; here he compared such humility to that of a servant (*diakonos*) or a slave (*doulos*). The possessive pronoun your in both cases is plural, implying that the great believer is servant or slave of all fellow believers. This is equivalent to saying, "The first will be last" (19:30; 20:16), but Jesus' words here were more graphic. The person who is genuinely great, by heaven's definition, is the one who chooses an attitude of submission to others in the family of believers.[9]

All of God's people are called upon to serve others. More graphically, it is fair to say we are called to be slaves in the service of God's Kingdom. This is NOT an appeal only intended for the Pastor or ministers. This teaching is laid upon all believers. Remember, Jesus said "my yoke is easy". Since this teaching is for all believers, how much more is it required for Pastors and deacons? Servants, ministers, Pastors, and deacons are all tied to the doctrine of slavery—**slave** (*doulos*). Pastors and deacons when chosen or elected for service are tied to serving, in some capacity

---

8   *The New King James Version* (Nashville: Thomas Nelson, 1982), Mt 20:25–28.
9   Stuart K. Weber, *Matthew*, vol. 1, Holman New Testament Commentary (Nashville, TN: Broadman & Holman Publishers, 2000), 324.

as a *doulos* (slave). No wonder that character, integrity, and humility are important concepts when choosing not only Church representatives, but especially important in selecting deacons and Pastors who are the faces of the local Church.

> All of Jesus' teachings assume that true humility is based on a healthy self-image. Only the person who is at peace with his true worth in God's eyes can act toward others without trying to prove his or her worth. Convinced of one's self-worth, the believer demonstrates this concept by attempting to demonstrate the worth of others (cf. John 13:1–17).[10]

Serving others is an honorable service before God. It is sacrificial in its nature. It demands maturity. It should never be a position of entitlement, or honorary like the Grand Marshal of a parade. It is a position of **WORK**. It is not for the lethargic, the procrastinator, the bitter or the lazy. [6] So we built the wall, and the entire wall was joined together up to half its *height,* for the people had a mind to work. (NKJV Nehemiah 4: 6)[11] Here, Nehemiah is praising the people, but it could and perhaps should also be applied to deacons. **Deacons need to have a mind to work.** Sitting in a deacon's meeting may be planning, but to call it service is stretching this Biblical concept a bit far.

In our present culture it is often considered menial and demeaning to be called a servant, to do service or to operate as a server. Servanthood, in Christ Jesus, is the spiritual basis for our Christian worldview, for it is **taught by Jesus, demonstrated by Jesus, and praised by Jesus**. Jesus took these words and breathed new life into them with HIS words and by HIS example and today, in our present age, we understand that Pastors and deacons are servants. This is supported by Scripture. Scripture DOES NOT limit the doctrine of "Servanthood" to only Pastors or deacons but should be embraced by all of God's people. The Church should be filled with servants. Sadly, all too often, ten percent

---

10   Stuart K. Weber, *Matthew*, vol. 1, Holman New Testament Commentary (Nashville, TN: Broadman & Holman Publishers, 2000), 324.

11   *The New King James Version* (Nashville: Thomas Nelson, 1982), Ne 4:6.

of God's people do all the tithing, all the praying and all the work. If you doubt this—ask a Pastor!

If we are to believe that the last days are upon us, then time is running out to catch God's vision for the Church.

Ancient Israel failed to realize their place as a Kingdom of priests[12] and a light unto the Gentiles[13]. These were not Israel's only transgressions, for Israel also ignored God's directive about the Jubilee and time of redemption and restoration. Israelites were to serve all of God's people. Yet greed, idolatry, and child sacrifice also impacted God's holy judgement on the nation of Israel. Taken together, Israel, as a nation, rejected their birthright just as Esau did. Although the Church is not a substitute for Israel; for God is **clearly not through with Israel**. The Church should learn from ancient Israel! If God would not withhold HIS judgement on Israel, the apple of God's eye[14], why would God withhold HIS judgement from the Church? We clearly see, in the early portion of the book of Revelation, that God stands ready to judge the local Church.

During the next sections we will examine key passages that deal with the doctrine of "Servanthood". We will examine Jesus' teachings, His example, and His praise of those with a servant's heart.

A woman praised for her service.

---

12   NKJV Exodus 19:6 **And you shall be to Me a kingdom of priests and a holy nation.'**
      These *are* the words which you shall speak to the children of Israel."
13   NKJV Isaiah 42:6 **"I, the LORD, have called You in righteousness, And will hold**
      Your hand; I will keep You and give You as a covenant to the people, As a
      light to the Gentiles, 7To open blind eyes, To bring out prisoners from the
      prison, Those who sit in darkness from the prison house."
14   NKJV Deuteronomy 32:9 **For the Lord's portion *is* His people; Jacob *is* the place of**
      His inheritance. 10 "He found him in a desert land And in the wasteland,
      a howling wilderness; He encircled him, He instructed him, He kept him
      as the apple of His eye.

Pharisees do not come across very well in most of the Gospels. Every now and then a Pharisee surprises us. In Luke 7 we have a Pharisee inviting Jesus into his home for supper. Though this was a good thing apparently, he wanted to hear Jesus, and then he quickly reverted to the kind of Pharisee most expect to find in the Gospels.

> NKJV Luke 7: 37**And behold, a woman in the city who was a sinner, when she knew that *Jesus* sat at the table in the Pharisee's house, brought an alabaster flask of fragrant oil, 38 and stood at His feet behind *Him* weeping; and she began to wash His feet with her tears, and wiped *them* with the hair of her head; and she kissed His feet and anointed *them* with the fragrant oil.**[15]

On one level we are repulsed with the idea of dropping to the floor and washing someone's feet with our tears especially when we realize that Jesus would have been walking around a city without modern day plumbing and in sandals. Nowhere else in the Gospels do we see this kind of devotion. This unnamed woman was clearly overcome by her emotions. Many of us have experienced a tremendous wave of emotions when we realized our need for Jesus. Luke does not tell what she was feeling nor what her emotional motivation was for doing what she did! Others have tried to explain her actions. While no one can know for certain, the following seems reasonable.

> The question spontaneously presents itself to us, what may have given occasion to this burst of feeling in the homage rendered by the woman. Without doubt she had previously seen and heard the Lord, and, in whatever way it may have come to pass, had already received a great benefit from Jesus. We are most disposed to understand this as a bodily healing and benefit, certainly not worth less than the debt of five hundred denarii. For this mercy she will manifest to the Lord her thankful love. Perhaps He had, in order to put her to the proof, delivered her indeed from the malady, which was the consequence of her

---

[15] *The New King James Version* (Nashville: Thomas Nelson, 1982), Lk 7:36–38.

sinful life, but as yet withheld the word of pardon and grace, of which she stood in most need. So there burns along with the flame of gratitude the secret longing after a higher, spiritual salvation in her heart. The impure wishes to be declared pure, the fallen to be raised up, the sorrowing to be comforted, the thankful for recovery to be blessed with yet greater fullness of grace. For a shorter or longer time, she has already been looking for an opportunity to draw near to the Savior without being thrust back by an un- compassionate hand, and now when she hears He is a guest in Simon's house, she is withheld as little by false shame as by fear of man from following the drawing of her heart.[16]

All we really need to know about this woman is the praise Jesus lavishes upon her. Jesus accepts her gift from her Alabaster Box. Jesus accepts her tears as the liquid to wash His feet and He accepts her hair as if it is of the finest linen. Jesus accepts her humble sacrifice as due HIM. Though some of the disciples begrudged her offering and some of the Pharisees despised her intrusion—Jesus willingly accepted her offering and used her actions to point to HIS coming death and burial; but the story does not end there.

Next, we see into the character of the Pharisee hosting Jesus.

> NKJV Luke 7: 39 **Now when the Pharisee who had invited Him saw** *this,* **he spoke to himself, saying, "This Man, if He were a prophet, would know who and what manner of woman** *this is* **who is touching Him, for she is a sinner."**

Clearly, the host knew this woman, and Luke provides some insight into the thinking of Jesus' host. Presumably, Jesus shared this later, or perhaps the host admitted to these thoughts later that night. However, Luke received this knowledge, we can know that no one can have

---

16   John Peter Lange and J. J. van Oosterzee, *A Commentary on the Holy Scriptures: Luke,* trans. Philip Schaff and Charles C. Starbuck (Bellingham, WA: Logos Bible Software, 2008), 122.

expected to have supper with Jesus without Jesus peering into his soul. Knowing this, Jesus did not immediately confront His host but began by asking HIS host a question, which was a typical approach any rabbi might have used.

> NKJV Luke 7:41 **"There was a certain creditor who had two debtors. One owed five hundred denarii, and the other fifty. 42 And when they had nothing with which to repay, he freely forgave them both. Tell Me, therefore, which of them will love him more?"**

The natural answer is the one who owed the most! (some have estimated that the price of the ointment that was used to anoint Jesus was valued at 300 denarii.) This was the Pharisee's reply to Jesus. A simple question and a simple answer. If only all questions and all answers were so easily done. The creditor's action would have been in the spirit of the Jubilee year. Jesus' host, as a Pharisee, would have known this and HIS host is given an opportunity to act in the spirit of Jubilee. Jesus, then as now, is never satisfied with just words, for deeds matter most of all. The context of this interaction is the year of Jubilee.

> NKJV Luke 7:44 **Then He turned to the woman and said to Simon, "Do you see this woman? When I entered your house; you gave Me no water for My feet, but she has washed My feet with her tears and wiped *them* with the hair of her head. 45 You gave Me no kiss, but this woman has not ceased to kiss My feet since the time I came in. 46 You did not anoint My head with oil, but this woman has anointed My feet with fragrant oil. 47 Therefore I say to you, her sins, *which are* many, are forgiven, for she loved much. But to whom little is forgiven, *the same* loves little."**

> 48 **Then He said to her, "Your sins are forgiven."**

The staging is important. The Pharisee answered correctly, then Jesus turns His back upon His host and speaks directly to the women. This woman would have been essentially invisible to everyone of moral character. Society would have shunned her. Judaism would have shunned her. The Temple would have shunned her as would the Temple Priest. And NOW she was being addressed by Jesus while all those who despised her were at Jesus' back and she was face to face with Jesus. Now Jesus accuses His host: you gave me no water to cleanse Myself, you gave me no welcome, you gave Me no anointing. All this Jesus deserved and had a right to expect. Then Jesus forgives her by saying: "**Your sins are forgiven.**" And the people gathered there wondered who Jesus was. Then Jesus says: "**Your faith has saved you. Go in peace**". In the home of the Pharisee Jesus demonstrated His power of insight, supernatural knowledge, a right to demand honor and the power to forgive sins. For our purposes we can see more! This woman presented herself in the most menial posture possible. She anointed Jesus, she cleansed His feet, she was drawn to Jesus, and she was praised for her service. Service is praised by Jesus. Let us all learn from this **un-named woman**. This woman was the only one praised in the house of the Pharisee.

More could be said here. Sermons and devotionals have focused on this passage down through the centuries. In this case a woman served Jesus and Jesus accepted her loyal devotion. We need to learn to be gracious enough to accept service or services rendered to us. When someone does something nice for us, let us be joyful and appreciative of their gift. It may be that we need to learn to be more loving and giving to others. It never hurts to be reminded that we can all be servants. All of us have a place to serve within the Kingdom of God. Serving the Kingdom is not limited to Pastors and deacons but opened to all believers. Come, let us serve God together, has been the motto of many houses of Worship.

Two examples of Jesus' service (Wine and the Towel).

We do not have many pictures, in the New Testament of Jesus' relationship with HIS mother prior to the beginning of Jesus' public ministry, but we do have this one. Just prior to Jesus' formal introduction to the world HE and HIS disciples were invited to a Wedding feast where HIS Mother was serving in a capacity of Wedding Planner. In the middle of the wedding celebration a crisis developed: the wine was gone but the celebration continued.

> NKJV John 2:1 **On the third day there was a wedding in Cana of Galilee, and the mother of Jesus was there.**
>
> **2 Now both Jesus and His disciples were invited to the wedding. 3 And when they ran out of wine, the mother of Jesus said to Him, "They have no wine." 4 Jesus said to her, "Woman, what does your concern have to do with Me? My hour has not yet come."**
>
> **5 His mother said to the servants, "Whatever He says to you, do *it*.**

What jumps out in this passage? 1, The wedding celebration is short on wine! 2. Jesus' mother seems to be overseeing the wedding provisions! 3, Mary has an expectation that Jesus will solve the problem. Mary, the mother of Jesus says to Jesus, "They have no wine!" She then says to the servants, "Whatever He says to you, do it." Whatever someone might say about this passage Mary had a great expectation that Jesus would resolve the immediate problem and that the servants would do whatever Jesus asked them to do. In this picture we see that both Mary and Jesus had authority.

How does this touch on deacon ministry? Mary is serving the Bride and Groom; Jesus is serving Mary and by extension the Bride and Groom, the servants are serving Mary and Jesus and by extension the Bride and Groom. There is a lot of serving going on. And all the serving is going on behind the scenes, this is a picture of humble service. Who, then, gets the glory? Not Mary, not the servants not Jesus! Who gets the glory? **The Groom, of course** and he does not know why!

> NKJV John 2: 9 **When the master of the feast had tasted the water that was made wine and did not know where it came from (but the servants who had drawn the water knew), the master of the feast called the bridegroom. 10 And he said to him, "Every**

man at the beginning sets out the good wine, and when the *guests* have well drunk, then the inferior. You have kept the good wine until now!"

The best servants are unnoticed and invisible to the guests. The best servants make the host and hostess look good. Chaos or difficulties should go unnoticed if the servants are doing their job. These are the best kind of servants. They are the unsung heroes and heroines of any event, function, or ministry. **Humility should be the Christian's watchword; how much more so for a deacon or Pastor?**

Much more could be said about this passage and it does warrant further study, but that is outside the purview of this book. NO Christian service is menial before God. All service has value when it is done to please God. To many times deacons and Pastors feel some jobs are beneath them. No job is beneath a Pastor or a deacon! especially when it is done for God's Glory or in the service of HIS Kingdom.

> **While serving as an interim Pastor in the Alabama Baptist Association, I asked deacons if they would assist me in serving tables. The idea was twofold: 1) our fellowship space was small and 2) the previous Pastor had severe difficulties with the current deacons. My thinking was that I and the deacons could be seen working together and we could alleviate the difficulty in moving around the fellowship hall. A few would make sure that everyone had enough to drink and reduce the flow of traffic. I was stunned at the reaction of the deacons who said, with almost one voice that serving tables was beneath them. I stood alone and served the tables by myself. Needless to say, I did not last long there.[17]**

In John 2 we see Jesus serving behind the scenes as did Mary, the mother of Jesus, and the servants of the household all joined in service. They participated in a miracle few knew about when it happened. They served behind the scenes and for all intents and purposes they were invisible

---

[17] This occurred in the late 1990's in Brookwood, AL.

to those that benefited from the miracle. This is one of the examples of Jesus that little "d" deacons should closely examine. Deacons who do not do minister but consider themselves as leaders and are entangled in the business matters of the Church completely miss what deacon ministry is about. Big "D" Deacons miss out on the blessings of ministry and are out of step with Scripture. Deacon ministry is not honorific! It is not a title to be cherished. It is a get your hands dirty and do the work of Jesus job! A little "d" deacon understands this. This is not a ministry for the aged nor for the squeamish. Little "d" deacons must be able to push a lawn mower, minister to hospice patients, visit nursing homes week after week! Little "d" deacons must have some stamina to do all of this and be at the Church whenever the doors open. The more we are like Jesus the better we minister to all people in the name of Jesus. Little "d" deacon ministry is hard. Jesus ministered to lepers; we must minister to all – even if they are infected with Covid-19, AIDS, or even Ebola!

Jesus and the towel!

In the previous example we saw several servants doing a variety of things behind the scenes to support a wedding celebration. In that case the servant's actions were invisible to the wedding guests. For Jesus, "In marvelous grace He came not to be ministered unto, but to minister", therefore, those who are humble in service and those engaged in the humblest service are nearest to Him. **This is their reward for turning their backs upon the honors and emoluments of the world.**[18]" In our next passage we have a public demonstration of Jesus' humble service.

> NKJV John 13:3 **Jesus, knowing that the Father had given all things into His hands, and that He had come from God and was going to God, 4 rose from supper and laid aside His garments, took a towel and girded Himself.**

Jesus removed his outer garments and prepared to work and now took upon himself the appearance of a slave (doulos). Today, we might say

---

18   Arthur Walkington Pink, _Exposition of the Gospel of John_ (Swengel, PA: Bible Truth Depot, 1923–1945), 87.

he took off HIS coat and tie, then rolled up HIS sleeves and set out to work. It is clear, Jesus was ready to work! Still talking about Jesus:

NKJV John 13: 5 After that, He poured water into a basin and began to wash the disciples' feet, and to wipe *them* with the towel with which He was girded.

This was not rinsing and drying the disciple's feet! There was some scrubbing to do, and Jesus was doing the scrubbing! Even a casual reader can see that Jesus was working hard at washing the disciple's feet. There must have been a lot of silence in the room or at most only whispers from one disciple to another. Likely someone said: What does this mean? Peter was probably preparing what he was going to say to Jesus when his time came. Peter's comments would be pre-meditated!

Imagine washing sandaled feet in a time before indoor plumbing.

While serving as a Chaplain at Fort Sill Oklahoma, my family (wife Marjorie and James and Joel) had the opportunity to go on a hike to see long horned steers and American Bison on the range. As we were walking along my youngest son was hopping from one rock to another. Then I heard him shout: "Soft rock"! I turned and saw him standing ankle deep in a fresh Bison patty. It is funny now, but not so funny then. We cleaned his shoes, which were now kind of green and I carried him on my shoulders while his mother got to carry his shoes. I had the heavier package but mine smelled better than what Marjorie carried. This is what I think of when I read about Jesus washing the Disciples' feet.

Jesus washed eleven pairs of stinky feet. Imagine that! When compared to this most Pastors and deacons have had it easy, maybe too easy. In the act of washing the Disciple's feet Jesus performed a service usually reserved for the most junior of servants. Others see deeper meaning in the act of washing the disciple's feet.

The rising from supper and the laying aside of His garments (cf. John 20:6) pictured our Lord on the resurrection-side

of the grave. The girding Himself speaks of service, the heavenly service in which He is now engaged on behalf of His people. It is a wonderful thing that the Lord never relinquished His servant character.[19]

Serving people is one of the examples Jesus left us. We are not to forget the widows, orphans, the sick, prisoners, the poor or the needy. We are to be concerned with all of these. Giving money to build institutions does not eliminate our responsibility to serve and minister to others. There is no substitute for going and doing! It is time to get our hands dirty as we seek to serve others.

CONCLUSION

No ministry is too menial, too dirty, too hard, nor too disgusting for Pastors and deacons to do if there were such a ministry who would do it? If it is ministry, then it is worth the energy needed to accomplish the mission. Every ministry is for God's glory and for HIS kingdom; because of this "highest good" no ministry is beneath anyone. Ministry is not sitting around a table discussing how money should be spent or if a new ministry should be started! Ministry is not talking about ministry. Ministry requires decisive action on the part of Pastors and deacons. Identification, preparation, mobilization, and implementation are all part of ministry because ministry is intentional. Ministry prepares both the minister (pastor and little "d" deacons) and the one being served for a Good News presentation. The Gospel can never be separated from ministry, how else will the one being served recognize whose name the service is in? Remember, we go where the LORD sends us. When we are sent by God the Holy Spirit has already paved the way for our service. Serving God glorifies the Son.

---

[19]   Arthur Walkington Pink, *Exposition of the Gospel of John* (Swengel, PA: Bible Truth Depot, 1923–1945), 707.

CHAPTER TWO

Origins of deacons

What does the word "deacon" mean?

T he meaning of the word "deacon" is really where the rubber meets the road, which makes this the crucial question in understanding the role of deacons in the local Church (see note).[20] What then is the meaning of the word " deacon "? How does the Bible define deacon? Bible translators have tried several approaches. Servant, minister, and deacon are the most common choices to translate the Greek word "διάκονος". Transliteration is a term used to describe what happens when a Greek word such as διάκονος, is changed from Greek lettering to English lettering, which in this case would be: **diakŏnŏs**, pronounced as: *dee-ak'-**on**-os. This is where translators have come up with the word deacon.*

Diakonos (deacon) is not used exclusively for men either. In one clear case the use of Greek: *diakonos* refers to a woman in Romans 16:1.

> NKJV Romans16: 1**I commend to you Phoebe our sister, who is a** *servant* **(*diakonos*) of the church in Cenchrea, ²that you may receive her in the Lord in a manner worthy of the saints and assist her in whatever business she has need of you; for indeed she has been a helper of many and of myself also.**

---

[20] Notice the author did not say today's Church or the modern Church or even the local Church. We are concerned with the Biblical understanding of deacons we are not concerned with definitions that change with the wind. The focus will be on: What does the Scripture say?"

The word "servant" is translated from the Greek work **διάκονος** which is of course is transliterated as *diakonos* where we come up with the word **deacon**. When Paul introduces "our sister Phoebe" as a *diakonos* "of the church at Cenchrea" (the same form is used for masculine and feminine)[21] the context suggests a similar formalized office within some local Churches. Historically when translators have translated ***diakonos it is usually translated as servant***. *Other times it translated as minister.* In a few instances ***diakonos*** is translated as deacon, signifying a formal office of serving males as far as the translators were concerned.

The Greek word ***diákonos*** *is most commonly a reference to a servant.* And for translators, s*ervant is the root word for deacon. We can see the evidence of this in the Book of Acts.*

> NKJV Acts 6:2**Then the twelve summoned the multitude of the disciples and said, "It is not desirable that we should leave the word of God and *serve* tables.** ³**Therefore, brethren, seek out from among you seven men of *good* reputation, full of the Holy Spirit and wisdom, whom we may appoint over this business[22]; ⁴but we will give ourselves continually to prayer and to the ministry of the word."**

The Apostles were not, in any way, implying that serving tables was demeaning. Their objections were that it was constraining and limiting their time for prayer and study. They believed this ministry was needful and they were looking for solutions on how to continue to carry out this ministry.

It is commonly understood that this is the first time "deacons" are formally called into service (Acts 6). Notice how the twelve apostles phrased the need. **"It is not desirable that we should leave the word**

---

21 Warren C. Trenchard, "Deaconess," ed. David Noel Freedman, Allen C. Myers, and Astrid B. Beck, *Eerdmans Dictionary of the Bible* (Grand Rapids, MI: W.B. Eerdmans, 2000), 325.

22 **"this business"** refers to serving tables **NOT** financial business of the Church as some deacons have suggested.

of God and _serve_ tables. The word "serve" used by the apostles is the Greek word diakonein. Notice how closely this resembles the word _diakonos_. Both the server and the serving are remarkably similar words, and this connects them together. This is the same word that Martha used to complain to Jesus that Mary was not helping in the kitchen (see Luke 10: 40 and following). Few if any scholars would dispute that deacon and servant are two intricately connected words used many times throughout the New Testament. The key point is our English word **"deacon"** is based on our English word servant/slave. Deacons are servants! **Deacons are not "titled"** like a Knight in England or a Duke or Baron. Deacons are servants doing a specialized ministry: **this is a ministry of the hands**.

A deacon in today's church is often taken/given as a title rather than a description of services provided. A Queen or King of England can confer the Title of Knighthood on an individual. In this case Knight Jones is a title conferred by Royalty. This is not the case in the New Testament when a local Church calls one of its own to be a deacon. A deacon, in the New Testament Church, is a description of an individual's duties rather than as a title. Returning to Acts 6, a need was identified, and men were appointed to fulfill that need and that specific need was described as "serving tables" in Acts 6.

A deacon in one local Church in Alabama once argued that deacons presided over all business of the Church, including the financial needs of the Church. As his proof he used Acts 6: 3 to support his claim.

> NKJV Acts 6:3 **Therefore, brethren, seek out from among you seven men of _good_ reputation, full of the Holy Spirit and wisdom, whom we may appoint over this <u>business</u>.**

He said, "See, right there it says BUSINESS!" The other deacons heartily agreed. It took a lot of patience and careful Bible Study to show that the business referred to was taking care of widows and orphans. To be honest, this issue was never really resolved at this Church.

The last example illustrates the need for all deacon ministries to be firmly rooted in Scripture. This is not a lesson to be lost on the local Church; every policy, procedure, activity, and ministry **must be firmly rooted in Scripture**. This will alleviate many potential problems in the future growth and development of the local Church.

In summary, the root word of "deacon" can refer to men and women. This is not in question by any scholar. Usually, the word that is sometimes translated as deacon, servant and minister primarily has the meaning of "one who serves". This is not a menial service, for all service for the Kingdom of God is **worthy service**. Service focused on glorifying God is never demeaning service.

Remember, our English word "deacon" is translated from Greek to English and the original Greek word can refer to either a man or a woman. In many Churches, up to the modern era, the **FORMAL** role for deacon was almost exclusively reserved for men although some exceptions do exist.

Is the ministry of deacon less important than the Pastor?

The short and simple emphatic answer is a deafening **NO!**

One of Jesus' favorite words was servant. HE referred to HIMSELF as servant on more than one occasion. This will be explored later. In the Old Testament there are many references to servant and more specifically to our interest is the phrase "Servant of the Lord". For example:

> **Servant of the Lord.** *A wonderful* Grand title applied to a variety of persons in the Bible. The basic term, *servant*, covers a range of meanings. Used some 800 times in the Old Testament alone, servant refers to a slave (with less stigma than in American history), to an officer close to the king, or to the chosen leader of God's people.[23]

---

[23]   Walter A. Elwell and Barry J. Beitzel, "Servant of the Lord," *Baker Encyclopedia of the Bible* (Grand Rapids, MI: Baker Book House, 1988), 1927.

The idea is that government officials serve the people with the approval and direction of God. This is akin to the idea found in the New Testament – under shepherd.

This simple phrase (**Servant of the Lord**) has a direct and powerful meaning to the ancient Hebrews, Jesus, and the New Testament Church. Regardless of where one fails in the social order, the divine importance placed on personhood is never questioned. People have status before God that no mere mortal has the right to tarnish. This is one reason that people of faith are staunch defenders of the Right to Life. Personhood is a divine right. It does not matter if one is a king, or a king's minister, or the lowliest slave. We all have an opportunity to have a relationship with God. Jesus reminded us in a powerful way about this very issue. Jesus said:

> NKJV Mark 9:35**And He sat down, called the twelve, and said to them, "If anyone desires to be first, he shall be last of all and servant of all."**

This teaching is found in all Gospels, not just Mark. At the Time of Jesus, there was Caesar; no one existed who rivaled Caesar in power or prestige; then senators; governors, mayors, right on down to slaves who also had various classes. Jesus inverted this top-down system. If you desire to be the greatest be like a slave – "**a servant to all**". Some may look down on a servant, but this is not a Biblical view. All of us are called to be **servants**. Servanthood was and is elevated by Jesus' teaching.

Jesus illustrated this by **HIS** personal example. In the first instance Jesus performed an act usually reserved for a slave or the youngest member in a household. For many this would be considered a menial job. Jesus did it with relish. **Do you remember the story?**

> NKJV John 13:5 **After that, He poured water into a basin and began to wash the disciples' feet, and to wipe *them* with the towel with which He was girded. ⁶Then He came to Simon Peter. And *Peter* said to Him, "Lord, are You washing my feet?"**

⁷Jesus answered and said to him, "What I am doing you do not understand now, but you will know after this."

⁸Peter said to Him, "You shall never wash my feet!"

Jesus answered him, "If I do not wash you, you have no part with Me."

⁹Simon Peter said to Him, "Lord, not my feet only, but also *my* hands and *my* head!"

¹⁰Jesus said to him, "He who is bathed needs only to wash *his* feet, but is completely clean; and you are clean, but not all of you." ¹¹For He knew who would betray Him; therefore He said, "You are not all clean."

¹²So when He had washed their feet, taken His garments, and sat down again.

Two things jump out of this passage: one, Jesus washed Judas' feet, and two, Jesus did a menial act and elevated it to a saintly act. **Please understand what is happening here.** Jesus is on HIS knees at the feet of each of HIS disciples (including Judas—the one who betrayed him) and one by one washes their feet on bended knee including the feet of one who would deny HIM, one who would doubt HIM, one who would betray HIM, two who sought power in Jesus' coming Kingdom and seven others who never really got with the program until after the Resurrection. **All of these had their feet washed by Jesus.** And all but John would flee once Jesus was arrested. Only John stood with Jesus until Jesus' death.

Until we can see the word **deacon** and **think servant,** we will not be able to grasp the importance of a deacon's role in a local Church. We must not allow ourselves to fall into the trap of a **BIG** "D" deacon but a little "d" deacon. We need servants in the local Church, not men with titles **who have forgotten** the meaning of **their role as servants.**

One more example of the attitude associated with humble servanthood. In this example we see another sort of foot washing. And we see the manner and form of Jesus' praise for another foot washer.

> NKJV Mark 14: 3 **And being in Bethany at the house of Simon the leper, as He sat at the table, a woman came having an alabaster flask of very costly oil of spikenard. Then she broke the flask and poured** *it* **on His head. 4 But there were some who were indignant among themselves, and said, "Why was this fragrant oil wasted? 5 For it might have been sold for more than three hundred denarii and given to the poor". And they criticized her sharply.**

> **6 But Jesus said, "Let her alone. Why do you trouble her? She has done a good work for Me. 7 For you have the poor with you always, and whenever you wish you may do them good; but Me you do not have always. 8 She has done what she could. She has come beforehand to anoint My body for burial. 9 Assuredly, I say to you, wherever this gospel is preached in the whole world, what this woman has done will also be told as a memorial to her."**

Here we have another foot-washer: this time a woman does the washing. Previously we saw whose feet Jesus washed now we see Jesus' feet washed. Those closest to Jesus focused on the money that she spent. It is interesting that the money spent was the woman's own money to be spent however she wished to spend it. She chose to spend it on Jesus. The disciples had no right to begrudge this woman's right to spend her own money. It is distressing to see how much time is spent in a business meeting focusing on how this little bit of money is being spent and how little time is spent on finding money to do ministry. Notice how Mark records those that criticized the women: "And they criticized her sharply". From the context it is completely reasonable to assume that ALL the disciples criticized the women. Notice Jesus' final comment: "Assuredly, I say to you, wherever this gospel is preached in the whole world, what this woman has done will also be told as a memorial to her".

This woman is still remembered for her service to Jesus. This prophecy is fulfilled every time this Story is told.

Neither Matthew nor Mark names this woman who washed Jesus' feet. She has gone down through time unknown and her name hidden in distant memory. Nevertheless, she is remembered, for Jesus reserved such high praise for very few and only this one woman has been given such an eternal memorial. It will be a fabulous day when we are privileged to hear this unnamed woman tell her tale. This woman may have been one of the very few of the humblest people to ever grace God's good earth with their tears and footsteps.

Who is most important in ministry: the one who plants or the one who waters? The apostle Paul gives us the answer.

> NKJV 1 Corinthians 3: 5 **Who then is Paul, and who *is* Apollos, but ministers through whom you believed, as the Lord gave to each one? ⁶I planted, Apollos watered, but God gave the increase. ⁷So then neither he who plants is anything, nor he who waters, but God who gives the increase.**

Sometimes ego gets in the way of ministry! Sometimes people claim credit although all credit belongs to God. It is always about God. The one who waters nor the one that plants are entitled praise, but only God who gives the increase deserves praise. The focus is not on the work but on God who gives the increase. We live in a competitive world, where praise is desired and bestowed, but this is not the way it should be in the Kingdom. **Kingdom living requires new Kingdom thinking**. Few really capture this key biblical concept. Big "D" deacons seldom realize the blessings found in serving others. Look at those who volunteer at feeding stations and the Joy that fills their faces as they serve the very kinds of people that Jesus served: the hungry, the sick, the despised and the unclean. We should do no less.

IN SUMMARY. Pastoral ministries and deacon ministries are not the same nor is one ministry superior to another. We minister as opportunities present themselves and as we are called. The apostle Paul put it best when he said:

NKJV 1 Corinthians 12:12 **For as the body is one and has many members, but all the members of that one body, being many, are one body, so also *is* Christ. ¹³ For by one Spirit we were all baptized into one body—whether Jews or Greeks, whether slaves or free—and have all been made to drink into one Spirit. ¹⁴ For in fact the body is not one member but many.**

All parts of the Church must work together for the Glory of God to be pleasing to our God of grace. This is the Biblical mandate. Let us endeavor to pray that all parts of our local Church work together to Glorify our Heavenly Father. May this be the prayer of every Minister, including Pastors, deacons, and Church members.

It is important to remember deacons are ministers too and their ministry is worthy of respect and admiration. A little "**d**" deacon ministry is a difficult ministry! Ministering to those in hospice, nursing homes, assisting the elderly in staying in their homes are all difficult ministries, some requiring hard labor.

In a practical way, what does this mean for deacons and their Pastors?

Ministry requires hours of prayer and Bible study. No ministry honoring God can be separated from Scripture or from prayer. When deacons are engaged in Biblical service the positive testimony of the local Church has a great impact on the local community. When deacons fail to meet the Biblical standards conflict between the Pastor and the deacons **will occur**! Of course, the same can be said in reverse. When conflict of this type occurs, the Church is left in a difficult situation. More times than not the Church will side with the deacons. When this happens, the Pastor is usually asked to resign. Churches have been trying to wrestle with this question for many years with varying success. The practicality of this hinges on a few key issues:

Pastoral failings
The Church and the Pastor are not a good fit.
Pastoral authority
    The Biblical role for deacons
    Church Growth
    Old big "D" deacons
    Change[24] (see note)

Sadly, Pastoral failings are all too common. In the United States Army Chaplaincy, it has been said Chaplains fail because of money, sex, or money. The idea is that money still corrupts. Chaplains have more access to large funds than most Baptist Pastors. In most Baptist Churches, for instance, the Pastor does not have an opportunity to misuse monies. Thanks to the many layers of committees, business meetings, and trustees. It is more likely that others in the Church will misuse Church funds. Churches where the Pastor controls the finances are a tinderbox ready for some complaint or accusation. More likely, the Pastor would succumb to a moral failing, allowing himself to be in some compromising position (innocent or immoral) or engaged in some immoral activity. This is much more likely than a Pastor misusing Church funds. A moral failing of a pastor damages the Church family and the Pastor's family. In a situation of a moral failure the best outcome is for the Pastor to resign. In lesser situations, such as, the Pastor was in a compromising situation, spiritual discernment is necessary. The reputation of a Pastor is of the utmost importance, as is the reputation

---

[24] I could share several stories and illustrations supporting my choices of issues within local Churches. These issues come from my personal experiences and stories from both Pastors and deacons. Many books, denominations and associations have programs to help resolve tension within the local Church. In my personal experience this is most keenly felt when the pastor has some moral failure. This is not the focus of this little book, except in a generalized fashion. Sometimes a pastor and a church are just not a good fit then a program to help resolve tension is indeed helpful often this is a waiting period for the pastor to find another position. Patience from the body of Christ is a way to minister to this pastor and his family. Remember the Church called the Pastor!

of the local Church. Remember, your Pastor can be a target of some sick individual (see note at the bottom of the page).[25]

In the situations presented before, deacons can be crucial in the healing process. And in both cases an Intentional Interim Pastor should be called to lead the Church through these types of situations. Deacons are strongly encouraged to research the Intentional Interim Programs that may be available through your denomination. A key point to remember, for an interim to be most effective, it should be understood from the start that he is not eligible to be the Pastor. Only then can he work to make ready the Church for a new Pastor. Additionally, go slow, do not be in a hurry to move on and remember patience is a virtue.

IN SUMMARY. Pastoral failings and when the Church and the Pastor are not a good fit are opportunities for deacons to demonstrate their spiritual maturity. In the case of moral failings, the Pastor must go, but it can be done in a loving way not only for the Pastor's family but also for the victim (and victim's family) as well. In this case of moral failings, the victim's (or their guardian's) feelings, needs and desires must be given every consideration. Including the need to contact the police. This should not be construed as legal advice. Laws vary from state to state as to what is required to be reported to the authorities. The Church may want to seek legal advice before proceeding if the Pastor had a moral failing.

---

[25] While on active duty at Fort Sill, Ok. I was the target of one such attack. I was at my office in a Chapel, near the front gate. This was pre-9/11 when public access was granted to many Army installations. An attractive woman came into my office and asked to speak to a Chaplain. My Chaplain assistant ushered her into my office. Unknown to me shortly after she came to my office my Chaplain Assistant was called to another building. This woman started taking off her clothes and I started to holler for help. Of course, none came. I was able to escape and ran outside and lucky for me two MPs were driving by and I flagged them down and all ended well for me. I am not sure what happened to the women.

Situations in which the Pastor and the congregation are not a good fit has its own sort of problems. In consultations with Churches and deacons who find themselves in this situation, the following is recommended:

1. Remember the Church sought God's guidance in calling the Pastor.
2. Was God wrong or is it more likely the pastoral committee and the Church were wrong?
3. The Pastor has financial needs and needs to be able to care for his family.
    A. Severance Package of at least one year that can be canceled when another position is found.

    B. Or one year to find another position.

A Pastor 's financial life should not be destroyed because the selection committee and the Church made a poor choice or because of some power struggle within the Church. Again, these are just general suggestions. It is important to remember how you treat your Pastor during a transition will impact who may be called following the transition. Other Pastors in your area will know how your Pastor was treated and they will talk about the Church. Reputation is important. When a Pastor is not a good fit remember he is one of God's chosen ministers, treat him with respect and grace.

Pastoral Authority

Who is in charge? This is a key concept concerning the leadership of the Church.

This has been touched on lightly, before. The position usually is based on the Church government of the local Church's denomination. Even so, some general principles still apply.

1. Christ is the head of the Church. Ephesians 5:23

2. Christ Jesus has appointed local shepherds. Jeremiah 3: 15[26] and Acts 20:28
3. Deacons serve under the direction of their Pastor. Acts 6
4. The Church calls the Pastor with the leadership of the Holy Spirit - **to lead the Church.**
5. The Church along with the Holy Spirit's leadership calls deacons for specific tasks to assist the Pastor.

The only one on the above list needing some explanation is item 3. Deacons serve under the direction of their Pastor after all **the Pastor is the shepherd of the whole flock, including deacons**. Big "D" deacons may treat their position as a title with power and prestige. In reality, the position of a deacon is to be a little "**d**" deacon where they treat their position in the spirit of servanthood as Christ taught the apostles. Prestige comes because of righteous service (see 1 Timothy 3)

Remember **a servant has no power and no prestige**; humility is expected. A more concrete way of understanding this Biblical concept is how we should introduce men who are deacons, for instance, "This is Mr. Jones he is one of our Church servants or this is Mr. Jones he is one of our servant deacons. Remember **deacon is a descriptor not a title**. Some Churches, when deacons are selected give the deacons a bowl and a towel as emblems of their position. Other Churches have deacons serving food and waiting on tables during Church socials and again demonstrating their servant role.[27]

---

[26] English Standard Version (ESV) Jeremiah 3: 15 And I will give you shepherds according to My heart, who will feed you with knowledge and understanding.

[27] This is a beautiful expression of Biblical servanthood. Although I have heard of and seen firsthand how some big "D" deacons adamantly rejected the suggestion that they should serve tables. The most important thing I have ever told a deacon is that they should always do their best to say yes to their Pastor. And secondly, I would add never talk negatively about your Pastor in public or in private. If you must do so have a deacon's meeting after you first tell the Pastor what your objection is and give him an opportunity to speak. The Pastor should never be excluded from a deacon's meeting. **Unless there is a compelling Biblical reason to do so**, such as when he is accused of a Moral failing.

The Biblical role for deacons.

What is the Biblical role for deacons? This is not an easy question to answer. Many answers have been attempted ranging from Pastor's Helpers to a Governing Body of the Church.

A careful reading of the Book of Acts leads most to the conclusion that the Six Greek Jews and one who was a Jewish proselyte from Antioch were presented before the Apostles were the first deacons. Most likely many in the Church would be surprised to learn that not all Bible believing Scholars hold the same opinion as most Bible believing Christians. Both views have some merit, but it is hard to escape that a careful reading of the stories of these seven men lead most to accept them as the first deacons. It is from this premise that we move forward.

Scripture references concerning deacons are few and precious and only Acts gives clear information regarding the duties and responsibilities. The apostle Paul spent more time dealing with the qualifications than with individual duties and this should be a clue how seriously the local Church should be in choosing deacons. From the Acts passage we see the following:

> NKJV Acts 6: 1 **Now in those days, when *the number of* the disciples was multiplying, there arose a complaint against the Hebrews by the Hellenists, because their widows were neglected in the daily distribution. [2] Then the twelve summoned the multitude of the disciples and said, "It is not desirable that we should leave the word of God and serve tables. [3] Therefore, brethren, seek out from among you seven men of *good* reputation, full of the Holy Spirit and wisdom, whom we may appoint over this business; [4] but we will give ourselves continually to prayer and to the ministry of the word."**

> [5] **And the saying pleased the whole multitude. And they chose Stephen, a man full of faith and the Holy Spirit, and Philip, Prochorus, Nicanor, Timon, Parmenas, and Nicolas,**

a proselyte from Antioch, [6] whom they set before the apostles; and when they had prayed, they laid hands on them.

The Message Bible is more dramatic in its telling of the same story of Acts 6 but, clearly the same message is being discussed.

> The Message Bible Acts 6:1 During this time, as the disciples were increasing in numbers by leaps and bounds, hard feelings developed among the Greek-speaking believers— "Hellenists"—toward the Hebrew-speaking believers because their widows were being discriminated against in the daily food lines. So the Twelve called a meeting of the disciples. They said, "It wouldn't be right for us to abandon our responsibilities for preaching and teaching the Word of God to help with the care of the poor. So, friends, choose seven men from among you whom everyone trusts, men full of the Holy Spirit and good sense, and we'll assign them this task. Meanwhile, we'll stick to our assigned tasks of prayer and speaking God's Word."

> [5-6] The congregation thought this was a great idea. They went ahead and chose—

> Stephen, a man full of faith and the Holy Spirit, Philip, Procorus, Nicanor, Timon, Parmenas, Nicolas, a convert from Antioch.

> Then they presented them to the apostles. Praying, the apostles laid on hands and commissioned them for their task.

Examining this passage more closely we can see how the deacon ministry began. Let us break down how this ancient ministry began:

FIRST: Some had their feelings hurt. This is not uncommon in Churches today.[28]

---

[28] I once encountered two ladies who would not worship together. They refused to be in the same building with one another. If they came to Church and saw their

SECOND: The Apostles identified the problem.

THIRD: A remedy was discovered, apparently by the Apostles

FOURTH: The remedy was presented to the Church.

FIFTH: The Church gladly received the remedy

SIXTH: The Church was involved in the process

SEVENTH: The Church choose seven men.

EIGHTH: The Apostles blessed the choices of the Church.

We can see by the above outline that the process was logical, deliberative, and respectful of people's feelings. Although, the emotions of those with hurt feelings did not seem to impact the resolution process. Unchecked emotions are not an asset during a business meeting they are a hindrance. We live in a day that Pastors are not treated with the same respect as they were in previous generations. And we find ourselves living in a contentious world, polarized politically and socially. Public forums are seldom a good place for civil discourse. Much of this behavior is/has been creeping into Church business meetings. When emotions are hot, little business is accomplished. Deacons can be either a disruptive force or a calming force in these situations. When deacons and the Pastor are united the Church will almost always joyfully follow. Emotions should never override the Bible or reason. When emotions dominate evil is given an opportunity to enter into the fellowship of God's people.

LESSONS LEARNED FROM ACTS 6: 1-6.

1. Deacon ministry arose due to a specific need within the local Jerusalem Church.
2. Deacon ministry was Church centered (focused on the Church membership).

---

enemy's car in the parking lot, she would turn her car around and go home. After speaking to both I am convinced neither remembered what the slight was.

3. The Apostles assigned (NKJV) or appointed (Message Bible) deacons for a ministry task.
4. Deacons were not in a leadership role.
5. No mention of a lifelong appointment.
6. No mention of ordination.
7. Deacons were not in charge of the business of the Church but over the ministry of widows and orphans.
8. Deacons were ministers in every sense of the word but were not administrators, leaders, directors, or business supervisors.
9. Deacons were well versed in Scripture.
10. Deacons were entuned with the Holy Spirit (Stephens preaching and Philip's evangelism).

IN SUMMARY: The Apostles appointed/assigned deacons to a specific task. They were not assigned in leadership roles nor in an administrative position. Deacons were called to focus on ministry. Deacons' meetings should be focused on ministry not on the business of the Church. Most Churches have people to do the business of the Church and if not, then perhaps the Church is not large enough to need deacons either.

CLOSING COMMENTS FOR CHAPTER THREE

If you have stuck with this little book about little "d" deacons, then you are at least open to considering looking at deacon ministry in a different light than most do in today's Churches. Likely you are interested in the local Church experiencing a Biblical Revival where God's people confess their sins at the altar of the Church. And Pleading with a Holy God to send a **Revival Fire**. There can be little doubt that when God sends a Revival Fire many others will flock to the Church to see why so many are so excited about Church.

Great Revivals have some things in common across the ages: One person begins to feel the heavy hand of God upon their shoulders to pray for revival. Next, they enlist others to pray. They rediscover the Word of God is worthy to be read and studied every day so that we are ready to receive a Word from God. Of course, it is true you do not have to pray or read the Bible to hear from God. But when we are praying and studying God's Word, we are at least in the frame of mind to hear a message from God.

> NKJV Romans 10: 14 **How then shall they call on Him in whom they have not believed? And how shall they believe in Him of whom they have not heard? And how shall they hear without a preacher?**

This passage deals with the mission field, but it seems it makes sense that we need to ready ourselves to be blessed with a Holy Revival Fire. This advice has been shared with many ministers: "Set the pulpit on fire preacher boy and stand back and watch it burn." We can rework this and say: Let us set our hearts on Fire and let us Fire up our attitudes and desires for communion with a Holy God. Revival Fire can come again!

The leader of the Church is the pastor, for he is the under-shepherd of Christ and has been entrusted with the mantle of leadership. Deacons are ministers not leaders. This means a division of roles is important to maintaining the integrity of ministry. Only when the ministry of a deacon is directly affected by the business of the Church should a deacon become entangled with the Church's business. Deacons should stay out of the business of the Church, especially the financial business. (more on this later).

True Story: The author was a voluntary staff member of a local Church, and following his confirmation he discovered the following:

> Deacon A's wife was the Church secretary.
> Deacon B's wife was the Financial secretary.
> Deacon B also received payment for serving as the Young Adult Minister
> Deacon C was employed by the Church to maintain the grounds.
> Deacon C appeared to be overly affectionate with Deacon A's wife and they lead a Sunday School Class together.
> Deacon D resigned then said he did not resign then resigned but said he did not really mean it.
> One of the above Deacons also served as chairman of the Finances.

Both Deacons B and C were being paid for services to the Church!

From the perspective of the author no deacon ministry existed, nor did anyone seem to be interested in doing deacon's ministry. It appeared that they were all Big "D" Deacons focusing on controlling the business of the Church[29] and destroying their Pastor or at the very least under mining the Pastor's authority. This process has been repeated at this local Church several times.

Pastors and deacons must have a **HIGH VIEW** of Scripture! This provides the freedom to do ministry for. the Bible is our mandate for ministry. If a high view of Scripture is important to us, then naturally we will have a Biblically based understanding of what the role of a deacon is. **The deacon's role is directly linked to service**. Jesus elevated the concept of servant to an important status symbol. We should not be ashamed or demeaned to be a servant in the Kingdom of God. We are, as believers, Kingdom citizens. Jesus glorified servanthood. Let us glory in serving the Kingdom of God and be found pleasing to God. It is far better to be a servant in God's Kingdom that being found outside the Gates of Heaven.

---

[29] I served a little over a year in the position, if memory serves, and seldom had a restful sleep during the time I served there. I had already submitted my resignation, when the deacons forced the Pastor to ask me to leave even before my resignation went into effect. When this happened, I literally jumped for joy and that night I had the best night sleep I had since before I had assumed the staff position. Even today I think back at how well I slept that night. At that time, I asked the deacons if they would confirm that they were not planning to let the Youth Pastor go and then ask the Pastor to leave. The Chairman of the big "D" deacons stated emphatically that he knew of no such plan. Less than three months later the Youth Pastor was forced out and three months later the Pastor was forced out. Record setting Baptisms, record setting Youth Programs and growing attendance suggest, that the dismissals of the Youth Pastor and Senior Pastor were more about who controls the Church rather than effective Ministry.

CHAPTER THREE

Old Testament Roots for little "d" deacons

The Bible at the time of the apostles was limited to what is commonly called the Old Testament. The apostles also had something we do not have and that was the living breathing testimony of Jesus Christ. It was out of the living breathing testimony of Jesus Christ that came the Gospels. The letters, comprising the rest of the New Testament tended to address more practical matters of Church governing. And a few books deal with history and of course we have the Book of Revelation – a view of the last days. The roots of the Old Testament can be clearly seen in the New Testament, the Church, and the ministry of New Testament believers, no one should be surprised because the early Church was almost one hundred percent Jewish. During the early days of the Christian Church, the Church was considered a Jewish cult. The Roman government also considered the Church a Jewish group and sometimes persecution was directed at both groups at the same time.

What can the Old Testament tell of us about deacons in the modern Church?

In the pages of the Old Testament there are two groups of men who bear a remarkable resemblance to present day deacons. They are not an exact match; however, some similarities can be seen in a careful reading and we can easily see the roots of deacon ministry within the Old Testament. One such group was Israel's judges who governed groups of families to free Moses from the labors of his office. The other group is in some ways more interesting, but much less is known about the School of the Prophets. We will look at these two groups and see what light they can shed on Biblical little "d" deacon ministry.

The men who lessened Moses' burdens.

It is important to remember that this group of men and New Testament deacons were not and are not the same. Deacon ministry is exclusively ministry oriented. While Moses' men were almost exclusively administrators. Even so, similarities do exist. Let us examine the Scriptures!

> (NKJV) Exodus 18: 12 **Then Jethro, Moses' father-in-law, took a burnt offering and** *other* **sacrifices** *to offer* **to God. And Aaron came with all the elders of Israel to eat bread with Moses' father-in-law before God.**
>
> **¹³And so it was, on the next day, that Moses sat to judge the people; and the people stood before Moses from morning until evening. ¹⁴So when Moses' father-in-law saw all that he did for the people, he said, "What** *is* **this thing that you are doing for the people? Why do you alone sit, and all the people stand before you from morning until evening?"**
>
> **¹⁵And Moses said to his father-in-law, "Because the people come to me to inquire of God. ¹⁶When they have a difficulty, they come to me, and I judge between one and another; and I make known the statutes of God and His laws."**
>
> **¹⁷So Moses' father-in-law said to him, "The thing that you do** *is* **not good. ¹⁸Both you and these people who** *are* **with you will surely wear yourselves out. For this thing** *is* **too much for you; you are not able to perform it by yourself. ¹⁹Listen now to my voice; I will give you counsel, and God will be with you: Stand before God for the people, so that you may bring the**

difficulties to God. ²⁰And you shall teach them the statutes and the laws, and show them the way in which they must walk and the work they must do. ²¹Moreover you shall select from <u>all</u> the people <u>able men</u>, such as <u>fear God</u>, <u>men of truth</u>, <u>hating covetousness</u>; and place *such* over them *to be* rulers of thousands, rulers of hundreds, rulers of fifties, and rulers of tens. ²²And let them judge the people at all times. Then it will be *that* every great matter they shall bring to you, but every small matter they themselves shall judge. So it will be easier for you, for they will bear *the burden* with you.

The first thing that jumps out is that the word "servant" is nowhere to be found! These men were not servants as our New Testament deacons are called to be. These men were administrators. Examining the wording we can see the word "judge" used a great deal. We also have the word "burden" as well. Being a judge is a great burden seeing that even judges must stand before an Eternal Judge in the last days.

What brought Israel to this place?

Up to this time the greatest man in Jewish History was Abraham, he was the father of the Jews. Prior to being known as Abraham he was known as Abram. His name was Abram when God called him to become the father of a great nation. Before God renamed him Abraham, during the time God was training him a terrible famine came upon the land that Abram was promised. This is recorded in Genesis 12.

> NKJV Genesis 12: 10 **Now there was a famine in the land, and Abram went down to Egypt to dwell there, for the famine *was* severe in the land.**

During this time of famine Abram's people were few. It was some time after he departed Egypt that God renamed him Abraham. Sarah and Abraham had, the son of Promise Isaac who had two sons of which Jacob was the son of Promise who had many sons.

In the later years of Jacob's life, another famine arose in the Promised Land like the famine in the days of Abraham. God uses days of hardship to refine those HE has chosen for leadership. During those desperate days Jacob led his extended family to Egypt and lived under the protection of his son – Joseph. But a time came when a new Pharaoh came into power. And the Bible tells us that there was a new Pharaoh who "no longer remembered Joseph nor Joseph's God". Many years had passed and during those long years God blessed Israel and she became a great people - a nation, living within Egypt: a nation within a Nation. The people of Egypt grew afraid of Israel for God had blessed Israel with many children.

In Europe, the years preceding 2018 saw a great influx of Muslims entering European nations who maintained their strong national identity. With this migration of young Muslim men, the face of Europe has been forever changed. Now, some European nations are feeling what the ancient Egyptians must have felt. They see their nations being forced to change to accommodate this new people group. They are acting in similar ways that the ancient Egyptians acted. Segregation is one method being used. Another is attempting to force the newcomers to embrace the morality of Western Europe. Recently, new laws are being put forth directly aimed at controlling Muslims. This is the kind of things that Egypt was doing to Israel. The parallels are clear. Of course, the European Nations have yet to force Muslims into labor camps, as the ancient Egyptians did to Israel. But to be fair to history, one European Nation (Germany) did so to Israel in the 1940's. History has a way funny way of repeating itself. But let us not judge Egypt to harshly and forget about other injustices that other nations (including our own) have done to others.

Returning to our text we can see connections relating to deacons. Look closely at the requirements for Moses' men. Re-read again, out load, our text and see how it feels to the ears, listening closely to the words used about the character of Moses' men. Reread verse twenty-one.

NKJV Exodus 18:21 **Moreover you shall select from all the people able men, such as fear God, men of truth, hating covetousness.**

We can see that this was a job exclusively for men. We may not like this exclusive nature of Jethro's advice, but it is what it is.[30] Moving on to what some might say is cultural bias, let us look very closely into this verse.

1. Select from all the people!

A through search was made of all the men. The family or tribe did not matter. If you recall how Saul or David was chosen as the king of Israel, then an understanding of how through the search must have been. On the other hand, men of character stand out. Good character is found in all layers of society. When character is the sole requirement, it is not hard to discover men of good character.

2. Able men.

The English Standard Version uses the same phrase **"Able men"** as does the New King James Version. The most common meaning would be "men of power," or "men of ability." Today's English Version (TEV) states that it means "capable men" (18:21) or "competent men."[31] The NKJV keeps the more flowery language. **Certainly, competent men or men of ability conveys the correct idea.** These men needed to have an innate ability to fulfill their mission. They needed to be mission driven with a keen sense of fairness!

---

30 I am not one of those men who are going to criticize the Bible for its choice of pronouns. I have a high regard for Scripture. Fashions may change, culture may change but God's word is timeless.

31 Noel D. Osborn and Howard A. Hatton, *A Handbook on Exodus*, UBS Handbook Series (New York: United Bible Societies, 1999), 441.

3. Fear God.

The more literally translation would be men who are "fearers of God." Various translations have been suggested, such as the TEV suggests: "God-fearing men" and another suggests: "men who have reverence for God" (Durham). Cultural considerations may also have to be considered for example: "men who obey and serve God[32] Those that have been immersed in the King James Bible know that "fear God" does not mean terrified of God, but rather have a deep and abiding reverence or a worshipful attitude toward God. God has used ungodly kings to discipline Israel. But Israel's kings who "fear God" are praised in Scripture. Being right with God is key to leading God's people. Being right with God is key to a joy filled life.

4. Men of truth.

Men who can both see truth and speak truth regardless of the circumstances: truth-tellers. Men who are not afraid to speak truth to powerful people.[33] Men like this are easy for others to trust them. Respect goes a long way, especially when the rulings of a judge may go against us. When we have respect for a judge, we can more readily accept a bad outcome.

---

[32] Noel D. Osborn and Howard A. Hatton, *A Handbook on Exodus*, UBS Handbook Series (New York: United Bible Societies, 1999), 441–442.

[33] While serving on Active duty as a Chaplain, while deployed, I found myself in a difficult situation. My Battalion Commander did something that I strongly felt was morally wrong. He had used his position and ability to provide himself comforts that other soldiers were unable to have. Knowing that in the past we enjoyed a mutual respect I felt I could speak to him on this matter. After much prayer I spoke to him. For his credit, he understood my concerns and very graciously asked my advice for what was to be done. I made a few suggestions of which none were accepted by him. But he did put his comforts to good use and to be fair, what he did and the way he handled the situation will always remind me of how fortunate I was to serve under so great a man as LTC Xxxxx. It was my great honor to serve under him. I served under much lesser men but none greater that LTC Xxxxx.

5. Hating covetousness.

And who hate a bribe is literally "haters of [illegal] profit" Other ways to render this clause are "who cannot be bribed" (18:21 The English Version) "men who are honest and will not accept bribes" Fox has tried to preserve the form along with the meaning: "men of caliber, fearing God, men of truth, hating gain."[34] Who would want a judge that would accept a bride? This is another way of saying these men would judge fairly between the rich and the poor as well as between the powerful and the weak. In America, Americans have a strong idea of fairness. No wonder that Politian's who accept brides are considered the most despicable in our society.

Character matters. It is how we decide on who to purchase a house from, the mechanic who repairs our cars, the Pastor we sit under and the person we want for our spouse. At one time, someone's word was as good as gold. That is not the case today. Nevertheless, character still matters. Martin Luther King is known for saying: "Let us be judged on our character alone". The Old Testament speaks a great deal on the importance of Character. Even people of poor character want a Mechanic to have a lot of character when he works on their car. Even in the day in which we live Character still matters.

IN SUMMARY

Character matters in the small and the big things of life. It mattered in Abraham's son Joseph's life; it mattered to the Prophet Nathan when he called out the powerful king David for murder; and it matters to God.

Before moving to the next section, "The school of the Prophets," let us look at the words of great men who held character in high esteem.

"Fame is vapor; popularity an accident; riches take wings. Only one thing endures, and that is character." —Horace Greeley

---

[34] Noel D. Osborn and Howard A. Hatton, _A Handbook on Exodus_, UBS Handbook Series (New York: United Bible Societies, 1999), 442.

J. P. Morgan was asked what he considered the best bank collateral. He replied, "Character."

Samuel Smiles reminds us that "to be worth anything character must be capable of standing firm upon its feet in the world of daily work, temptation and trial; and able to bear the wear and tear of actual life. Cloistered virtues do not count for much."

An open manner of life is a person's best safeguard against slander.[35]

Character still matters.

The School of the Prophets[36]

There is extraordinarily little known about these men and possibly women of the Old Testament. It seems reasonable that these schools developed around personalities. In our world great men of charisma lead in the founding on some of our most famous Colleges and Universities. We see men and women like these in the pages of both Testaments. Samuel in the OT and Paul in the NT are two such personalities.

We know a great deal about Samuel and Paul through their writings. And they both had powerful magnetic personalities. A great personality may get people to turn their head and consider what you have to say, but to keep and hold them you must also have substance. The leaders of those ancient Schools of the Prophets are familiar names to both Jews and Christians: name like Samuel, Elijah and his successor was Elisha.

Although very little explanation is given to us directly from the Scriptures, we can gain some understanding about them. We can read between the lines of Sacred Scripture and make some reasonable assumptions about

---

[35] Herschel H. Hobbs, *My Favorite Illustrations* (Nashville, TN: Broadman Press, 1990), 30.

[36] In my younger days in the ministry, I confused the "sons of the Prophets" as literal prophet's sons and the School of the Prophets as OT Seminaries. I feel so sorry how God's people silently endured my early messages.

this group of Godly men who desired to learn the deep things of God. These men and possibly some women separated themselves from the cares of this World. We see in the life of Jesus that Jesus chose to take time and separate Himself from the close associations with others and focus on a time of renewal with God, His Father. We see this in the life of John the Baptist as well. Pastors and some Churches in our day see a need for a time of renewal for their Pastors and many Churches have realized a renewed vigor in the preaching of their Pastor when He returns from a time of personal reflection.[37] The desert, the closet, or the mountain top offer some kind of separation for renewal.

The Desert was, from the time of Moses to the days of John the Baptist, the great school of the prophets. These men of God were trained for their work:

1. By being brought face to face with their sacred mission in all its greatness, and free from the prejudices and petty influences of human society. There they could steadfastly contemplate the Divine ideal, undistracted by the rude realities of man's fallen condition.
2. There they were also cut off from all human aid, left to test their own strength, or rather to prove their own utter weakness, and, overwhelmed with the sense of it, to cast themselves wholly on Divine strength. Thus, they received directly from God, as did Elijah, the supplies by which they lived, and realized the conditions of absolute and immediate trust in Him. Coming forth from this discipline of the desert, they were enabled to say with Paul, "When I am weak, then am I strong" (2 Cor. 12:10).
3. This loving converse of the prophets with their God brought them into closer fellowship, more intimate union, with Him.

---

[37] My last Church blessed me with a 30-day time of renewal on my first year there and continued the practice for every year I served there. I benefited and the Church benefited. While I was away, I renewed myself at the well and returned refreshed and spiritually renewed. This is one area deacons can help their Pastor. Deacons I encourage you find the funds and the way to do this for your Pastor.

Thus, they came forth from the desert, like Moses from the Mount of Sinai, bearing unconsciously upon them the reflection of His glory[38]

A time of separation requires discipline and silence, but the rewards cannot be under-estimated. Ministering is enjoyable and rewarding but it is also stressful and spiritually draining. Deacons also need to have a disciplined time with God. This is one of many very important lessons we can learn from the School of the Prophets.

The Sons of the Prophets and the School of the Prophets are used interchangeably. These School may or may not have been formal institutions but seems more likely that they were not formal. Like deacons and Moses' men a specific need arose for a School of the Prophets. "The *schools of the prophets* are now again mentioned (1), though their historical connection with the association of prophets in the time of Samuel cannot be proved. It is probable that they were revived by Elijah, for the purpose of providing a kind of religious fulcrum for the people who were cut off from the lawful sanctuary and worship at Jerusalem, and of raising up men who would labor for the quickening of their spiritual life.[39]"

Remember these school arose under the prophet Samuel during a time chaos in Israel. Chaos during the reign of king Saul, chaos during the reign of king David and chaos prior to building the Temple of God.

Now we have some background for who the School of the Prophets were. Now let us examine some passages of Scripture pertaining to the School of the Prophets and see if deacons have any ancient roots reaching into the "School of the Prophets.

---

[38] H. D. M. Spence-Jones, ed., *1 Kings*, The Pulpit Commentary (London; New York: Funk & Wagnalls Company, 1909), 416.

[39] Gustav Friedrich Oehler and George E. Day, *Theology of the Old Testament* (New York; London: Funk & Wagnalls, 1883), 392.

NKJV 2 Kings 6 **And the sons of the prophets said to Elisha, "See now, the place where we dwell with you is too small for us. ² Please, let us go to the Jordan, and let every man take a beam from there, and let us make there a place where we may dwell."**

So he answered, "Go."

³Then one said, "Please consent to go with your servants."

And he answered, "I will go." ⁴ So he went with them. And when they came to the Jordan, they cut down trees. ⁵ But as one was cutting down a tree, the iron *ax head* fell into the water; and he cried out and said, "Alas, master! For it was borrowed."

⁶So the man of God said, "Where did it fall?" And he showed him the place. So he cut off a stick, and threw *it* in there; and he made the iron float. ⁷Therefore he said, "Pick *it* up for yourself." So he reached out his hand and took it.

This is a lovely story. You have no idea how beautiful this story is unless you have been part of a building program. If you have, then you know how precious it is when the people have a mind to build for God. King David had a mind to build a temple for God, but God knew the hands of David were bloody hands. King Solomon was the king that was given the task for building the Temple. These students had a willingness to build. Praise God for students with this kind of mindset. Seminary graduating classes often fund raise to build a bench or plant a few trees to leave for the next generation. But Elisha's students were extraordinary, the desired to build a new School from the ground up. Now that is one special class of students. Why would the students be so moved to do this? Dr. Moody may have put his finger on the reason why!

Now this reveals something of the popularity of Elisha. He taught in a theological seminary, the school of the prophets. The school grew, and they needed larger quarters. This was due to the presence and the popularity of Elisha.

Dr. Moody continues with the key ingredient to this school success. (highlights by the author).

The strength, I feel, and **the value of any school is the character and the ability of those who teach. It is not the methods but the men that are important**, especially in a Christian school[40]

If Dr. Moody is correct and surely, he must be then surely teachers of God's word must endeavor to ever reach a higher standard. Especially to his or her students. No greater memorial for a teacher can be than this: My teacher taught me a great deal and loved me while I learned.[41]

Elisha's students initiated a plan with Elisha's blessing and built a new school. How many students Elisha had is unknown? Many is more likely than a few. Notice the language of the text: "and let every man take a beam from there and let us make there a place where we may dwell" how many beams does it take to build a house for we do not know what manner of construction was being used. Nor do we know how big the beams must have been. How big of a beam can you carry? The point is that the students had a heart and the will to work. Today we would simply say they showed tremendous initiative. What would the Church be like if the people if the deacons and if the Pastor showed that kind of initiative. Thank God for our Church members that see a job that needs doing and goes right out and does that job.[42]

---

[40] J. Vernon McGee, *Thru the Bible Commentary*, electronic ed., vol. 2 (Nashville: Thomas Nelson, 1997), 315.

[41] Three professors did this for me: Dr. Bryan and Dr Cooley both from Samford University and Dr Chuck Kelly from New Orleans Baptist Theological Seminary.

[42] A few years ago, while I was planning and researching this little book, I was told the story of a rural Alabama Church. This Church only saw its Pastor on Sunday Morning and Wednesday Evening and an occasional fifth Saturday Singing. The Church was small, and the people did not have a local Pastor. One Sunday as the Pastor drove up to the Church the one and only deacon was there to meet him. The Pastor had a difficult work week at his secular job. The deacon said, "Preacher we have a leaking roof". The Pastor felt the weight of the world fall upon him. The deacon then said," Pastor what's wrong?" For the Pastor thought of all the costs and expense and extra hours it would take

As the students were cutting down the trees one of the iron axe heads flew off the handle and into the River Jordan it went. Here is another point that is key to the story and key to the understanding the students. Most students are poor. Ministerial Students are especially poor. And so, it was in Elisha's day. These students did not have tools of their own but had gone out and borrowed tools. These students were hustling to get the job of their new School up and running. Obviously, they were hard working and diligent students.[43]

In this passage you have the miracle of the "diligent students;" the miracle of the "hardworking students;" and the miracle of the resurrected axe head. Miracle come easily when the people have a heart and a mind to do Kingdom work. Little "d" deacons have a heart and a mind for serving others. Those with a heart and a mind to work for God see that great things can be accomplished. We see this theme in many places in scripture. We see it when the wall of Jerusalem needs to be repaired. We see it in king David's heart when he desired to have a Temple built for God. We have seen it in the lives of past generations who worked hard to build many of our Churches. Many Churches are debt free because of the many Saints of God who proceeded us to Glory. This is a great lesson that these early theological students can teach present day little "d" deacons.

---

to replace the roof. The Pastor said, "Don't worry about me Brother deacon, we will find a way to fix the roof". "Pastor," the deacon said, "I already fixed the roof, I just wanted you to know that it cost the Church $46.50." I am sure all Pastors would like to have a bunch of deacons like that.

[43] My wife teaches school, I would what she would say if next semester all her students were hard working and diligent in their studies. I know evenings at home, during the school year, would improve. I have a friend who was one of my professors while I attended Samford University in Birmingham, AL. He told me that he was asked to teach a night course. He said teaching that night course made him decide to retire following that semester. Students can be rough on teachers. Even on the absolute best of teachers. I have seen Sunday School teachers be treated horribly by their students. This is a problem in the Church. Let us love all teachers for they surely need it.

IN SUMMARY

Students with a plan of action, a willingness to work and a great desire to study the deep things of God built a Theological place of study. WOW. Deacons need to follow their example and focus their time as deacons for Biblical studies and service. Little "d" deacons will find a way to do both. God will bless you for your study and for your service. Service without Biblical support will likely lead you toward weariness and bitterness. Therefore, we need strong spiritual men to take on these greatly needed ministries.

CONCLUSION FOR CHAPTER THREE

When the first seven deacons were prayed over in Jerusalem the Bible was the Old Testament. They did not have benefit of the Bible we hold in our hands. At that time, the Gospels had not been written and the apostle Paul did not exist. In fact, a young man known as Saul was there when Stephen one of the first seven deacons was martyred for Jesus. The first Christian martyr was a deacon. For deacons Stephen was your ministerial forebear. Stephen is one of your ministerial ancestors. This is a staggering understanding of the importance of your position as a deacon in your local church. Therefore, the word "deacon" garners such respect within the Church. Deacons, as persecution continues to spread, will still be serving right alongside their Pastors—these will become the first targets of mass persecution.

Additionally, the roots of deacon ministry are deeply rooted in the Old Testament. It is easy to connect deacons to Moses' men and to the School of the Prophets. Moses' men and the School of the Prophets are not the same as deacons though they do have a similar reason for their birth. They were birthed out of a great need. Moses' men were needed to start a judicial system of the incredibly young nation of Israel. The School of the Prophets were birthed out of a spiritual need to teach God's people during a time of unrest and chaos. Deacons were birthed out of another need. A need of such importance that it formed an ignition switch for the first Revival in the early First Century Church (more about this later).

Let us remember, there is a continuation from the Old Testament to the New Testament. Deacons did not just magically appear out of thin air; they have a history! The apostles searched the Scriptures and inquired of God. This is only reasonable. The Church today is connected to the First Century Church. We are the Church of God (not the denomination) but universally. We are connected to the Church in Korea and Indonesia too. We are connected to the suffering Church in Africa and in Syria. Many of these Churches have deacons. Imagine how a deacon is received in Indonesia, Syria, Iran, or China. Death is their near future. Deacons should be the first to be praying for the persecuted Church. They are on the front lines. Forget about Missionaries as wonderful as they are, but they leave when the nation they minister in goes crazy. But the Pastors and deacons are left behind. In a persecuted nation after the Pastor is taken, they then come for the deacons. Think on this when you desire the office of deacon.

Heavenly Father, please extend your hand over all deacons and for those deacons that serve in persecuted lands may they serve well and if called to do so, die well. And may their last breath be pleasing to you. God have mercy on us during these wicked days. Strengthen our Churches that we may give a good accounting on what you have entrusted us with. In the name of Jesus, we pray. Asking and believing firmly in YOUR sure mercies.

CHAPTER FOUR

WHO do the deacons work for and who do the deacons answer to?

TWO CONTROVERSIES

Most people are opposed to controversy, and this is understandable. In the United States we have been anything but united on social issues including abortion, gay marriage, freedom of expression, freedom of association, gun rights, illegal immigrants and taxes. These are just a few things that divide the "un" United States. This little book will likely be considered controversial and opposed by Big "D" deacons and some Pastors. And the author welcomes oppositions to this little Book. The purpose is to call Churches to revival, by focusing on bringing God's Churches and their deacons to where they are in line with Scripture. When people and Churches become complacent, hearts grow cold. Then, when change is needed most, people and Churches resist the urgently needed change. The prophets in the Old Testament faced this kind of opposition, especially the Minor prophets like Amos and Malachi. John the Baptist also advocated for change and any casual New Testament Bible reader can easily see that Jesus challenged the religious elite at every opportunity. This little book is advocating for a lot of change. Some might argue that it is too much change in too short of a period. Change is hard and usually painful. When we are confronted with a Biblical necessity for change the response of all of us should be: "WE CAN DO THIS!" Two passages of Scripture come to mind when controversy was a good thing. The first passage deals with young king Josiah.

NKJV 2 Kings 23: 3**Now it came to pass, in the eighteenth year of King Josiah, *that* the king sent Shaphan the scribe, the son of Azaliah, the son of Meshullam, to the house of the Lord, saying: ⁴"Go up to Hilkiah the high priest, that he may count the money which has been brought into the house of the Lord, which the doorkeepers have gathered from the people. ⁵ And let them deliver it into the hand of those doing the work, who are the overseers in the house of the Lord; let them give it to those who *are* in the house of the Lord doing the work, to repair the damages of the house—⁶ to carpenters and builders and masons—and to buy timber and hewn stone to repair the house.**[44]

If anyone has any doubt to the value of reading God's word, then the life story of good king Josiah should remove any doubt.

Returning to the text. Here is a very young king Josiah. Obviously, he had a godly upbringing. He saw the Temple of God was in poor repair, so he ordered an accounting of the money that was collected over the years and held within the Temple treasury. Churches should be doing this too: monthly, quarterly and/or yearly. Back to the Text. We see in verse four that the Temple Treasury was growing fat and unused, so much so, that the building was in desperate need of repair. Following the accounting, the funds were ordered to be freed and delivered to those hired to do the repairs. This is all very straightforward and well and good. Many Churches have large bank accounts. That money needs to be released for Ministry. There are all kinds of reasons not to do it. But if we believe that the RETURN OF THE KING is imminent or the final days are upon us, then what good is money in a bank account?

Repairs were speeding along, and a great discovery was made.

NKJV 2 Kings 22: 8**Then Hilkiah the high priest said to Shaphan the scribe, "I have found the Book of the Law in the house of the Lord."**[45]

---

[44]   *The New King James Version* (Nashville: Thomas Nelson, 1982), 2 Ki 22:3–6.

[45]   Josephus, and of the Jews generally—that it was a copy of the entire Pentateuch. (So De Wette, 'Einleitung in das Alt. Test.,' § 162 *a;* Keil, 'Commentary on

Two thoughts come to mind: first, it would be great if the local Church would rediscover the Word of God and secondly, what kind of power would be released in the local church if God's word were more sought out than fried Chicken on Wednesday night?

How is it possible to lose one or all the first five Books of the Bible?[46] Likely none of us can fathom how it is possible to lose such a significant portion of Scripture. But they did, somehow! How long it had been lost is unclear. One thing is certain: they could not have faithfully done all that was required of them without the Word of God to lead and direct them. Now the long-lost Books of God have been discovered and the reaction of king Josiah reflects his closeness and openness to the Holy Spirit of God. Here is king Josiah's reaction!

> NKJV 2 Kings 22:11 **Now it happened, when the king heard the words of the Book of the Law, that he tore his clothes. [12] Then the king commanded Hilkiah the priest, Ahikam the son of Shaphan, Achbor the son of Michaiah, Shaphan the scribe, and Asaiah a servant of the king, saying, [13] "Go, inquire of the Lord for me, for the people and for all of Judah, concerning the words of this book that has been found; for great *is* the wrath of the Lord that is aroused against us, because our fathers have not obeyed the words of this book, to do according to all that is written concerning us."**

We do not need Biblical scholars to tell us what this means. Josiah sent a team of emissaries to inquire of God what it is that they must do, now that they have heard the words of God's Book. King Josiah knew, instinctively, that the Hand of God's judgement was hanging by a thread over the nation of Israel. Israel should have been the Priesthood/ Missionaries for the whole World, but they have forgotten the words

---

Kings,' pp. 477, 478; Bähr, 'Commentary,' vol. vi. p. 257; and others) H. D. M. Spence-Jones, ed., _2 Kings_, The Pulpit Commentary (London; New York: Funk & Wagnalls Company, 1909), 437.

[46] This author has no idea, how it is possible to lose one of the Books or all of the Books comprising the Torah.

of God. The Western World is almost in the same position that Israel was under king Josiah. Fortunately, there are still great men of God, standing in the gap, shouting the Word of the Lord to a desperate people living within a desperate nation. We all should feel encouraged at the increase of Godly street preachers. Like the great men and great women of our day, that still proclaim the Living Word of God, there existed in Jerusalem a great woman of God, by the name of Huldah[47]. What then did these ambassadors sent by king Josiah to the King of Glory discover from the prophetess?

> NKJV 2 Kings 22: 16 **"Thus says the Lord: 'Behold, I will bring calamity on this place and on its inhabitants—all the words of the book which the king of Judah has read—[17] because they have forsaken Me and burned incense to other gods, that they might provoke Me to anger with all the works of their hands. Therefore My wrath shall be aroused against this place and shall not be quenched.'"**

For a moment, take the time and think about what these men were thinking when the prophetess Huldah spoke these words. They must have looked at one another and thought: who wants to volunteer to take this message to the king? Then the prophetess Huldah spoke again.

> NKJV 2 Kings 22: 18 **But as for the king of Judah, who sent you to inquire of the Lord, in this manner you shall speak to him, 'Thus says the Lord God of Israel: "*Concerning* the words which you have heard—[19] because your heart was tender, and you humbled yourself before the Lord when you heard what I spoke against this place and against its inhabitants, that they would become a desolation and a curse, and you tore your clothes and wept before Me, I also have heard *you*," says the Lord.**

---

[47] In my mind three Old Testament Women stand out head and shoulders above the others and are underrepresented in the preaching and teaching of the Bible: Huldah, Deborah, and Rahab.

Key here, is the tender and humble heart of king Josiah. God links the tender and humble heart of the king to the saving grace of God. Huldah spoke of the Grace of God. We can be certain that all the men who came to Huldah's door breathed a sigh of relief when they heard these words. They must have felt joy tinged with relief for the good news they would now carry. With this good word from God, they returned to the king almost certainly with a glad and joyful heart. When a soul enters into the grace of God, their face changes, and observers can see a change come over them.

Next, the king puts the feelings of his heart into action.

> NKJV 2 Kings 23 **Now the king sent them to gather all the elders of Judah and Jerusalem to him. ²The king went up to the house of the Lord with all the men of Judah, and with him all the inhabitants of Jerusalem—the priests and the prophets and all the people, both small and great. And he read in their hearing all the words of the Book of the Covenant which had been found in the house of the Lord.**
>
> **³Then the king stood by a pillar and made a covenant before the Lord, to follow the Lord and to keep His commandments and His testimonies and His statutes, with all *his* heart and all *his* soul, to perform the words of this covenant that were written in this book. And all the people took a stand for the covenant.**

Revival in Israel broke out, first the king and then the Israeli leadership and then the people of Israel. This is what happens when God's people are serious about the Word of God. The revival in King Josiah was top down driven. This is what happens when the Word of God take precedence in the leaders of our Churches, in our lives and in our homes. Revival Fires begin to break out.

Have we forgotten why we looked at 2 Kings 22 and 23? It was because controversy can sometimes be a good thing. Sometimes controversy will cause us to look closely at our situation and move us from inactivity to activity. **Controversy,** within the Church should send us running to the Scriptures instead of allowing emotions to rule the heart. It was actions by the king rather than emotional energy that awoke a revival fire in ancient Israel. God says in Isaiah: [18] "Come now, let us reason together, says the LORD. [48] God reasons with us and only at the last resort does HE drive us with emotions. We see Jesus' reasoning with HIS disciples when He drives out the money lenders in the Temple with emotional energy.

THE SECOND CONTROVERSY

The second controversy we will examine is found in the New Testament book of Acts, recorded in Chapter 11. This early controversy within the early Church led missionaries to be sent to the Gentiles. Now, that is a good thing! Sometimes controversy motivates us to an important action.

> **NKJV Acts 11 Now the apostles and brethren who were in Judea heard that the Gentiles had also received the word of God. ²And when Peter came up to Jerusalem, those of the circumcision contended with him, ³saying, "You went unto uncircumcised men and ate with them!"**

Peter returns from a trip to the Gentiles (that would be us), and those of the circumcision (that would be the Jews), accused Peter of violating his Jewishness. The formerly wishy-washy Peter would have none of this and the apostle Peter told them of his vision, gifted to him by God, instructing him that Gentiles are worthy of the Gospel of God. Peter then tells them how the Glory of God filled their hearts with the love of God. The result of the controversy was the beginning of evangelism for the Gentiles (which is us). Up until this time the Church was almost exclusively Jewish and now the Church began to move toward evangelism.

Some controversies are good, and some of these controversies are resolved by a direct intervention from God. God's direct intervention with Peter settled the Gentile question forever for the apostle Peter.

---

[48]   *The Revised Standard Version* (Oak Harbor, WA: Logos Research Systems, Inc., 1971), Is 1:18.

Returning to the initial point. This little book is and will be controversial in many quarters. However, that does not mean it should be set aside. Remember, REVIVAL is the goal of this little book. In a similar manner, like in the days of Josiah, may the REVIVAL of our Churches ignite from among the servant-deacons of our Churches. Here in the United States, a national revival is desperately needed; a worldwide revival is also greatly needed. Pastors (including this author) have failed to move our nation—to kindle a Revival Fire.

In most of the Western Nations, God has been forgotten in the Capitals of once Missionary-sending nations. Our political leaders, like the political leaders of all the other Western Nations, seem to be spiritually bankrupt. Perhaps the last hope we have of a National Revival must come from the laity – the Lay ministers – the deacons. In the book of acts the appointing of the first seven deacons and their early ministry ignited a revival. In Acts 6, notice how this passage explains what happens next:

> NKJV Acts 6: 6**whom they set before the apostles; and when they had prayed, they laid hands on them.**
>
> 7**Then the word of God spread, and the number of the disciples multiplied greatly in Jerusalem, and a great many of the priests were obedient to the faith.**

Seemingly the ministry of the Jerusalem Church was being watched by the Jewish priests; perhaps some elements which were involved in the persecution of Jesus. They were so touched at how the Church ministered to the desperate that they too were moved to embrace the saving grace of Jesus. How believers conduct themselves really matters; not only how it touches those in need but **touches those who have seen a need and did nothing**. A Church in a building program, often experiences a growth because people see that something is happening, and they want to be a part of something exciting. Churches that are stepping out in ministry experience growth: not only because of those they help but also because a Church member tells those outside of the Church what their Church is doing. Church members will talk to people if there is something to talk about. Everyone enjoys talking about exciting things; that is why Churches involved in exciting ministry attracts working believers.

Deacons can make something happen for the Lord by being ready and obedient to hear what God has to say. Some deacons, feeling caught or trapped doing administrative work, could speak to the Pastor about some specific ministry that could be done: feeding programs, clothing ministry, caring for the lawn of one of your Church widows. Even a small ministry can touch a heart in a big way. And when her neighbors ask who was cutting her grass, she will say: "That was one of our great deacons at MY Church.

WHO DOES the deacon WORK FOR?

Take two points if you answered: for God and for the Church! Of course, these are the correct answers. Little "d" deacons serve both God and the Church. We could also put it this way: Little "d" deacons serve the Kingdom of God. We would be hard pressed to do better than that. In practical matters how does this work out? Try answering the following questions.

> Thinking of the deacons in your Church, what kind of picture comes to mind? (servant/minister or administrator (committee chairman))

> What are they known for doing?
>> Are they touching lives?
>> Are they leading committees?

> When you see your deacons what are they doing?
>> Praying in worship or teaching Sunday School?
>> Leaving a deacon meeting or touching people in direct ministry?

Here is the million-dollar question, what should they be doing?

These are not easy questions, and they are not meant to be. Defining the role of deacons is not an easy task. However, we do know some things about what they should be doing. And we do have information about two deacons in the Book of Acts: Stephen and Philip. These two men were extraordinary deacons. Surely, they must not be unique. Hopefully, all believers have heard some great stories about little d deacons – serving deacons. Praying that God will bless HIS Church with great deacons. Men with humble and tender hearts, like king Josiah.

An in-depth discussion about Stephen and Philip will be discussed later but suffice it to say for now they were **spiritually powerful men of God**. But a few things need to be shared here. Both deacons **witnessed for God**: one's witness was so profound that a man was saved on the spot (actually in a chariot, more likely a carriage of some type) and the other's testimony was so powerful that he was murdered because of his words. Both were in excellent health. Both men had a **strong grasp of God's Holy Word**. Both had a thorough **knowledge of Jewish History**. Both were singled out in Scripture. They were two of the first seven deacons. They were both committed to the Cross even unto death. And both men were **supernaturally used by God**. Probably there are more commonalities than these; but these are enough to see that these two deacons, at least, were special (however, this author does not believe they were or are unique).

In practice, the deacon works for the Church. We see two specific jobs they were assigned in the book of Acts: to care for the widows and orphans. They were responsible for purchasing and distributing food to the widows and orphans. Seems likely that an orphanage was developed and administered by the early Church and that these first deacons were responsible for that ministry. It would be hard to imagine that Christian children roamed the streets and then came to the Church to eat and the Church failed to put a pillow under their head.

Deacons minister in the local Church, but this is not to mean that they have no impact outside the Church (more about their impact in the closing pages). Perhaps the most effective way deacons can have an impact outside of the Church is when those they serve begin to praise their deacons in the public square (in the office, in the schools and in the local community). Word spreads when God's people are doing God's work.

WHO DOES the deacon ANSWER TO?

Two points if you said, "God and the Pastor". The Pastor is the under shepherd for the Church. Pastorates that are long are more stable and realize more growth than other Churches.[49] It takes time, 5 – 7 years, for a Pastor to gain the complete trust of the people and the deacons. A Pastor's ego may fool him if he thinks he is immediately trusted by all his people and all his deacons. One Pastor shared that it took 7 years before he felt that he could begin to make significant changes in how the Church did business. Long term Pastors have developed a bond with the people, and they have the trust of the deacons and the informal leadership of the Church. Churches who have a rapid turnover in Pastors (one every seven years or less) usually fall into one of two

---

[49] Pastor Knox Johnson and his wife Ruth was the first Pastor that took a serious interest in me. Throughout some difficult times. When the day filled with worry God always reminded me of this faithful couple who prayed day and night for me and my family. While I was deployed, as an Army Chaplain, I knew they were praying for my ministry and my safety. An encourager can do wonders for a broken spirit facing spiritual difficulties. Brother Knox taught me more about the Pastorate than all the years at Samford, Seminary and beyond.

Deacons be an encourager to your Pastor. I guarantee you it will be appreciated and remembered and talked about. I also guarantee you that your Pastor will brag on you, with other Pastors.

Another encourager I had was Brother Thomas and his wife Mary. These two taught me all you could know about evangelism. Encourage your Pastor and if he is young in ministry teach, he what you know. Your encouragement will never be forgotten. I have never met a Pastor that had too much encouragement.

categories: small Churches that cannot support a full time Pastor, or Churches that have a history of an unbiblical strong big "D" deacon Board where deacon is more of a title rather than the Biblical model of a servant. Big "D" deacons have an almost impossible time in any transition from a Big "D" deacon to a little "d" deacon ministry. Think of it this way, Big "D" deacons are like Pharisees, very few Pharisees were able to make the transition from Judaism to Christianity, though some did. This is a very difficult job for Pastors: to lovingly pray and patiently explain the joys of being a little " d" deacon whose focus is on serving God's people through the model provided by a Servant Messiah. Another Pastor shared the following, "For many years I prayed for the Deacon Board to move from administrators to active ministry. After receiving no inkling of change this same Pastor began to pray: "Lord please remove these men so that ministry can be done". Rapidly the old, styled deacons were gone, and real growth was realized in numbers and spiritual growth.

Generally, Deacons have reacted in a hostile way when they have been informed of their relationship regarding Pastoral authority. Deacons are ministers too, but there is a division of labor and a division of a calling. This is not a difficult concept to grasp. The problem comes when the power and/or prestige of the individual deacon is in danger of diminishing. Jesus gives us illustrations of shepherds and sheep that impact this wrongheaded way of thinking: deacons are servants, not men of power! And we have Scripture to support this claim.

Isaiah the prophet uses Shepherd imagery to describe the coming Messiah.

> NKJV Isaiah 40: 11 **He will feed His flock like a shepherd; He will gather the lambs with His arm, and carry** *them* **in His bosom,** *And* **gently lead those who are with young.**

This is a sweet picture of Christ Jesus pastoring His people. If we have been a Christian for very long, we can remember that we too have experienced the love of a Pastor: the love of an under-shepherd. There is a wonderful story about the difference between the shepherd and the butcher that illustrates caring and drive.

> **Who Drives and Who leads the Sheep:** A party of tourists was on its way to Palestine and its guide was describing some of the quaint customs of the East.
>
> "Now," said he, "you are accustomed to seeing the shepherd following his sheep through the English lanes and byways. Out in the East, however, things are different, for the shepherd always leads the way, going on before the flock. And the sheep follow him, for they know his voice."
>
> The party reached Palestine, and, to the amusement of the tourists, almost the first sight to meet their eyes was that of a flock of sheep being driven along by a man. The guide was astonished and immediately made it his business to accost the shepherd.
>
> "How is it that you are driving these sheep?" he asked. "I have always been told that the Eastern shepherds leads his sheep."
>
> "You are quite right, sir," replied the man. "The shepherd does lead his sheep. But you see, I'm not the shepherd, I'm the butcher." —*Church of God Evangel*[50]

This is a cute story unless you are the sheep. But the point is remarkably simple; the sheep follows the shepherd. Deacons are sheep as well as the congregation and have a need to be shepherded. When sheep follow the shepherd, all is well.

The demands for a Pastor's time can be enormous. This applies to bi-vocational Pastors, Interim Pastors, evangelists, and deacons. REMEMBER, DEACONS ARE MINISTERS TOO. This may

---

[50] Paul Lee Tan, *Encyclopedia of 7700 Illustrations: Signs of the Times* (Garland, TX: Bible Communications, Inc., 1996), 498–499.

be the most important lesson in this book. And it is a crucial one. Deacons can multiply many times over the impact of the pastor. Find ways to praise your Pastor at work. It is rare how seldom this is done.[51] Not everyone can lead like General Douglas MacArthur or General George Patton. Deacons pray for the Pastors leadership skills, perhaps with deacons praying the Pastor will grow into his job[52]. Pray for his discernment of spiritual things. Prayer makes a difference all the time and is needed even more so when there is tension within the Church. Deacons who support their Pastor in prayer find it easier to stand up for their Pastor.

Let us now turn and be specific as to our topic: **WHO DOES THE DEACON WORK FOR?**

Logically it follows that deacons are servants and servants need to know what the most important action is to be done. No one knows this better that the local Pastor. People talk to the Pastor in confidence. And needs are unknown to most, if not all, people. For instance, most Churches have hungry members. Most Churches have members who are lost, although they are on the Church rolls and attend Sunday School religiously. Most Churches have members who rarely feel the human touch except at the doctor's office. Most Churches have very

---

[51] I was asked to do some consulting for a local Church. The Pastor and deacons had developed some tension. The deacons were challenged to praise their Pastor at work in front of their co-workers every day! Within a week the tension was gone. Within a month attendance increased. I have asked Church members if they recall hearing of a pastor being bragged on by a co-worker. So far, I have never seen a hand go up. I have stopped asking because I was too discouraged. Deacons, brag on your Pastor in public. Do not be a run down the Pastor deacon, be the guy that says I have a great Pastor, and sound like you mean it when you say it and while you are at it, tell you face to smile too. A final word here, **I have never had a smiling deacon hurt my feelings**.

[52] Two cents again, I guess you would like me to up the ante. In every Pastorate I learned how to walk with God better and how to be a better Pastor. I thank God for the many godly people who helped me grow, even when I did not want to. I recently met a dear Pastor in Port Charlotte, Florida. Talking and sharing with him, impacted this little book. I thank him for his time and his heart's desire to Pastor his people.

lonely members, some are likely chronically depressed. A Pastor needs to have the freedom to direct his deacons in this way.[53] Deacons engaged in ministry need encouragement and direction. Feedback is necessary. Some deacons are more like utility players, others may be specialized. It takes pastoral leadership to direct the servant resources.

> Abraham's service was marked with *humility*. He bowed to his guests (Gen. 18:2), called himself a servant (18:3, 5), and called the feast only "a morsel of bread." He served the three visitors and then stood near to be available if needed. He interrupted a comfortable afternoon nap to become a servant to three strangers; but because of that service, he received tremendous blessings for himself and his wife. *(many scholars believe he was ministering to the pre-incarnate Son of God – Jesus)*

> Finally, he served the Lord *cooperatively* and involved the ministries of others. Sarah baked the bread; a young man dressed the meat; and no doubt other servants brought Abraham the butter and milk. "I would rather put ten men to work than do the work of ten men," said evangelist D.L. Moody; and he was right.[54] Deacons who are willing to work are more valuable that a pocket full of GOLD to a good Pastor.

In July 2018, the following sign was posted at a Burger King in Fort Myers, Florida. It read as follows: "HELP WANTED FOR THOSE WILLING TO WORK ! ! !". Pastors want deacons who are willing to work. Sunday School Directors, Vacation Bible School Directors want people who will work. Burger King wants people willing to work. A boss can hire a hundred people who will phone it in, but it is extremely difficult to find a hard and diligent worker. Anyone being considered

---

[53] The last deacons meeting I led, I asked for all the deacons to share what kind of ministries they have been involved in during the last month. It was the longest five minutes I have ever experienced. That was the moment I decided to explore writing a book about deacons and how they can ignite revival in the local Church.

[54] Warren W. Wiersbe, *Be Obedient*, "Be" Commentary Series (Wheaton, IL: Victor Books, 1991), 75.

to become a deacon should already have a strong work history within the Church. Lazy deacons are worthless distractions and hinder the ministry of God.

Servants of God can do a great deal for God when they are focused on the Kingdom of God. Abraham, the Father of Jews, understood what it meant to be a servant. He knew how to serve. In our culture many have forgotten how to be gracious and how to serve others. Humility is a forgotten virtue. Serving others has become "who will serve me". Deacons who have the zeal to be a servant in the kingdom of God are precious. Deacons, as you serve as a little " d" deacon, let your number one prayer be "Lord, let me serve your people with joy and gladness!" Serving is only a blessing when it is done without bitterness. Pray, brothers, Pray.

God loves to Shepherd HIS people. We know that Christ is the Good Shepherd. Look closely and the following references pertaining to God as our Shepherd.

> **God as Shepherd.** God who has been my shepherd (Gen. 48:15);
> the Lord is my shepherd (Ps. 23:1);
> shepherd of Israel (Gen. 49:24; Ps. 80:1);
> he will keep Israel as a shepherd keeps his flock (Jer. 31:10);
> he will tend his flock like a shepherd (Isa. 40:11);
> he leads his people like a flock of sheep (Ps. 78:52);
> you led your people like a flock (Ps. 77:20);
> you who lead Joseph like a flock (Ps. 80:1);
> he is their God, and they are his flock (Ps. 95:7; Ezek. 34:31);
> they are the flock of his people (Zech. 9:16);
> the sheep of your pasture (Ps. 74:1; Ps. 79:13);
> I will shepherd my sheep (Ezek. 34:12);
> be their shepherd (Ps. 28:9);
> shepherd your people (Mic. 7:14);
> I will shepherd my flock (Ezek. 34:15);
> [the Messiah] will stand and shepherd his flock (Mic. 5:4);
> he will make his flock, Judah, like a battle horse (Zech. 10:3);

awake, sword, against my shepherd, the man who stands next to me (Zech. 13:7);

out of Bethlehem will come a shepherd for Israel (Mic. 5:2–4; Matt. 2:6);

parable of the good shepherd (John 10:1–5);

I am the good shepherd (John 10:11; John 10:14);

one flock, one shepherd (John 10:16); the great Shepherd of the sheep (Heb. 13:20);

the Shepherd and Guardian of your souls (1 Pet. 2:25);

when the chief Shepherd appears (1 Pet. 5:4);

the Lamb will be their shepherd (Rev. 7:17);

you will shepherd them with a rod of iron (Ps. 2:9).[55]

If someone is having a hard time being shepherded, then perhaps that person is not a sheep. If someone is having a hard time being shepherded, then perhaps it is a time for self-reflection. If someone is having a hard time being shepherded, then perhaps they are a wolf in sheep's clothing.

Oh, my goodness, look at the references about God being our Shepherd, we see them from Genesis to Revelation! Look at the many reminders we have that we are the sheep and God is the Shepherd. Remember how powerful it was when we first heard Jesus say, **"I am the Good Shepherd!"** We can rejoice that the Good Shepherd, knows HIS sheep. It is good to be a sheep known by the Master Shepherd. There is nothing to be afraid of when we are a sheep in a land of coyotes while Jesus is our Good Shepherd.

If one will consider the emblem of nations. We can see, tigers, lions, and birds of prey as symbols of the nations. It interesting that the God of the Universe, God who holds all power and all wonders in HIS hand, chose a meek lamb to be the symbol of HIS people!

The Bible also has references to shepherds that God will provide to HIS people. We are precious to God and HE gives us shepherds. Everyone

---

55   A. Colin Day, _Collins Thesaurus of the Bible_ (Bellingham, WA: Logos Bible Software, 2009).

needs a shepherd. Sometimes shepherds come in the form of kings, like David; sometimes in the form of judges, like Deborah; sometimes in the form of a priest, like Eli; sometimes in the form of a prophet, like Nathan; and sometimes in the form of a good man called to be a Pastor at the local Church. Most of us with a little gray hair have had several Pastors who had strengths that other Pastors did not have. Pastors are called to lead Churches every bit as much as they are called to preach. The Bible supports this claim. There are many references for God being as a Shepherd and we can also see there are many references of others who have served as a shepherd.

People shepherding people: David will shepherd Israel (2 Sam. 5:2; 1 Chr. 11:2; Ps. 78:71);
they will have one shepherd, David (Ezek. 34:23; Ezek. 37:24);
I commanded [the leaders of the tribes] to shepherd Israel (2 Sam. 7:7);
where is he who brought up out of the sea the shepherds of his flock? (Isa. 63:11);
Cyrus is God's shepherd (Isa. 44:28);
shepherds and their flocks will come against her (Jer. 6:3);
seven shepherds and eight leaders against the Assyrian (Mic. 5:5);
they will shepherd the land of Assyria with the sword (Mic. 5:6);
he will separate them as a shepherd separates sheep from goats (Matt. 25:32);
I will give you shepherds after my own heart (Jer. 3:15);
I will raise up shepherds to tend them (Jer. 23:4);
tend my sheep (John 21:16);
he gave some to be shepherds [pastors] and teachers (Eph. 4:11);
shepherd the church of God (Acts 20:28);
shepherd the flock of God (1 Pet. 5:2);
who tends a flock without using the milk? (1 Cor. 9:7);
the wind will sweep away all your shepherds (Jer. 22:22);
where is your beautiful flock? (Jer. 13:20);
shepherd the flock doomed to slaughter (Zech. 11:4; Zech. 11:7);
collected sayings given by one shepherd (Eccles. 12:11).[56]

---

[56] A. Colin Day, *Collins Thesaurus of the Bible* (Bellingham, WA: Logos Bible Software, 2009).

God's Pastors are HIS under-shepherds. They are called and serve at HIS pleasure and at HIS bidding. Serve your Church well and a deacon will serve his Pastor well. Take care of him and his family financially. It is far better for a deacon to go the Finance Committee than the Pastor. If your Pastor is having to beg for coins from the finance committee, then your Church and the deacon have failed your Pastor. Deacons, we have looked at how the first deacons were specifically directed to do a specific job. But we did not discuss the "two whys" that precipitated the need for a deacon ministry. This is important for the relationship between deacons and the Pastor.

The first why was some women and likely orphans were not receiving their daily allotment for food. **Jesus said, "It is written, '*Man shall not live by bread alone,* but by every word of God.'"**[57] Deacons were to be entrusted with the bread. No one who has known want and hunger would suggest a full belly is not needed. This feeding ministry would have been in great demand in a place like ancient Jerusalem. Anyone remotely familiar with the New Testament would know that Jesus fed the hungry. Jesus performed miracles with just a few pieces of bread. These deacons would be following in Jesus' footsteps. **And now for the second why!**

> NKJV Acts 6:1 **Now in those days, when** *the number of* **the disciples was multiplying, there arose a complaint against the Hebrews by the Hellenists, because their widows were neglected in the daily distribution.** [2] **Then the twelve summoned the multitude of the disciples and said, "It is not desirable that we should leave the word of God and serve tables.**

The apostles were not claiming that serving tables was not a valuable ministry or that it was beneath them. The apostles were speaking from a position of authority about what is best for the apostles to do. The community of the faithful realized that the apostles needed to focus on prayer and study. One of the most important duties of a deacon is to protect his Pastor's time that is needed for study and prayer, otherwise

---

57   *The New King James Version* (Nashville: Thomas Nelson, 1982), Lk 4:4.

weak and ill prepared sermons will be the result. In a very practical sense, deacons are to protect the Pastor from himself. This seems silly to most people. However, a good sermon requires a great amount of time for Bible study, prayer, and research. The interesting stories your Pastor uses on Sunday mornings, Sunday nights and Wednesday evenings do not usually come as a direct Revelation from God. They usually come from study. Preparation is not always easy, and the Pastor must do his prep work while taking calls and between visits to the hospital. Remember, most Pastors do not have the luxury of an Associate Pastor helping with constant interruptions. The clear majority of Pastors do not even have a secretary who can run interference and screen the Pastor's calls. Now, with the advent of the cellphone, Pastors have even less privacy. Every member of the congregation can reach out to the Pastor at any time, day or night. Therefore, deacons need to care for their Pastor. Just as a deacon is also a member of the congregation (sheep) the Pastor is also a Church member and falls under the deacon's responsibility to minister to their Pastor. Deacons protect the Pastor from the Church and from himself. When deacons are actively engaged in protecting the Pastor, the congregation will receive better messages from a rested Pastor. Deacons should ensure the Pastor has an uninterrupted day off. Time to attend his children's' ballgames and activities at their schools. Pastors are often parents too.

Look at Acts 6 again.

> NKJV Acts 6 **Now in those days, when *the number of* the disciples was multiplying, there arose a complaint against the Hebrews by the Hellenists, because their widows were neglected in the daily distribution. 2 Then the twelve summoned the multitude of the disciples and said, "It is not desirable that we should leave the word of God and serve tables.**[58]

Again, notice very closely that there are two problems here, not just one. Earlier we looked at the two whys! Remember, the apostles had a need, and the Hellenists' widows had a need. The newly formed band

---

[58] *The New King James Version* (Nashville: Thomas Nelson, 1982), Ac 6:1–2.

of deacons solved both problems. They protected the apostles time and they provided for a need within the community of faith.

Pastors can be as dumb as a rock when it comes to worldly things (The author, as a Pastor, totally agrees). Pastors can allow their time to get away from them (This author has been told many times by a deacon to go home and spend time with my family; I thank God for that deacon). If a Pastor is receiving pressure from some elements of the Church, he will feel a greater need to spend more time doing Church work – longer work hours, more office hours and such. If your Church has a lot of older members, he may not even have a day off due to a needed emergency hospital visit or time to prepare for a funeral. If you have never been a part of preparing for a funeral, then likely you will have no idea how long it takes. This is not the time to speak about sermon preparation, other books have done that. But the Church is unaware of the mental and spiritual toll that a funeral has on their Pastor. Imagine praying for healing for weeks on end, then the Church member dies. Now comes meeting with their family members, who may or may not be Christians. This takes a toll on the Pastor. In most cases, only the wife of the Pastor understands how much this costs your Pastor. Deacons have many opportunities to minister to their Pastor. By taking care of the Pastor, deacons also minister to the Pastor's wife and to their children. Deacons can also minister to the children of the Pastor by acting like a great uncle to the children. Usually, Pastors are some distance away from their family and a pretend Uncle would be a nice blessing for their children to have. Children need extended family. Deacons can make their Pastor's family life so much more beneficial.

In preparation for this book, I have spoken to several Pastors whose children are no longer attending Church and I have spoken to the children themselves who are no longer in the Church. Every one of them, to date, mentioned how badly their father had been treated by his deacons. Deacons need to be forever mindful that when a Pastor comes under attack, his family feels under attack as well. How deacons handle Church tension has eternal consequences for the Pastor's children.

Pastors have been threatened with bodily harm by deacons. Pastors have received threatening letters, even long years after they left a given Church. Some Pastors had to involve a lawyer to protect them against all kinds of personal attacks. This happens much more than Churches realize. Deacons (!), as more of the world enters the Church, are needed to protect their Pastor more than ever. Protecting the Pastor also protects the Church's reputation. In our current political and social situation, the Pastor's reputation and the Church's reputation are bound together. It does not take a genius in public relations to imagine the headlines.[59]

Listed below are some helpful hints for both Pastors and Deacons:

> No private female counseling without another woman sitting outside the Door.

> (Nowadays Pastors and Deacons should consider having a male and female who are unrelated to the counselee sitting outside the door.)

---

[59] Personal testimony time, once again. While serving as an Intentional Interim Pastor at a Baptist Church I had all the things mentioned happen to me. I also received a threat that I would be killed if I Baptized one of the Youth. This one came from the girl's mother who was to be baptized. The mother later, told me, after I reported the threat to the Post Office, that she did not want her daughter baptized but did not want her daughter to know that it was her mother's idea to stop the Baptism. I once told a Church member he was not eligible to be a deacon and he later told me he wanted to leap across the table and strangle me. Seminary never prepared me for these kinds of reactions. I have been threatened by two different deacons at two different Churches to do me physical harm. All of these issues could have been resolved had the Chairman of deacons called out bad behavior. I have been in many deacon meetings, as pastor, staff, and as a guest and in none of those meetings has one deacon ever called out another deacon. The Pastor was left to tote the baggage instead of deacons disciplining themselves or Deacons need to police themselves to hold themselves accountable. This is the greatest weakness among deacons. Deacons must be willing to holding themselves accountable. If the Pastor is left to discipline a deacon, in a small Church or a Family Church it would be almost impossible to have a positive outcome. In a medium Church, it might take years to recover. But only in a large Church have I ever heard of a positive outcome of this kind of discipline.

(The Counseling Room should have a window in the door that will give a full room view.)

(A panic button should be in both the Counseling Room and the Pastor's Office.)

No private Hospital Visits. Other Family members should be present, or better yet, visit in teams.

When visiting the Hospital alone LEAVE THE DOOR OPEN or PRAY FROM THE DOORWAY.

Be wary of traveling with anyone who is not your spouse or on the Ministry Team.

Be sensitive to your spouse's concerns.

You should never tell your spouse any Church secrets.

Few Pastor's spouses and few Deacon's spouses are equipped for Biblical Counseling. Spouses let the deacon be the deacon and let the Pastor be the Pastor.

Be aware of your surroundings.

NEVER VISIT SOMEONE WHO IS HOME ALONE. Bring company.

If your Church does not have other staff on hand, work from home.

These are some basic issues that other Pastors and some deacons and at least one spouse shared with the author. These hints/suggestions have evolved from real life experiences. Protecting reputations is the responsibility of the one who values his/her reputation. There are no shortcuts when reputations are on the line.

Deacons typically have a longer tenure at their Church than does the Pastor. Sometimes it works the other way but not often. Deacons can save a Pastor's ministry by insisting on some guidelines about counseling. Sexual harassment claims are being leveled at men of position, power, and wealth routinely. If the Pastor has taken strong public stands in the media, he is in danger of attack. Simple guidelines and a few basic protocols will go a long way in protecting your Congregation from those that HATE the Word of God and target your Pastor. Deacons, help protect your Pastor.

SOME FINAL WORDS FOR DEACONS AS WE CLOSE THIS SECTION: Pastors can be hard-headed when it comes to doing counseling. This is an essential ministry but protect your Pastor from being reckless. Insist on some agreed-to guidelines. Do this with all aspects of ministry.[60] Protect your Church volunteers by ensuring all the doors to all the classrooms have full view windows. Take a full security assessment of all programs and ministries especially, ensuring no false allegations will ever have merit. Take precautions now.

IN CONCLUSION: Deacons were given a specific job to do caring for the widows and protecting the Pastor's Bible Study and Prayer life. Later we will look how this list can and should lengthen. Deacons, love and pray for your Pastor and his family. Prayer is the most important thing any deacon can do for his Pastor. And second to this is for the deacons to strongly support their Pastor.

---

[60] Author tossing in his two cents, once again. Even now that I am no longer in the Pastorate, I will not ride in an elevator alone with a woman other than someone on the ministry team or a family member. With social media, such as it is, don't risk your reputation. Or the reputation of your Church. I believe that God is and will be calling more and more Christians to take public stances, I have done so. And I expect it is inevitable that the media and private organizations will increase public assaults on Ministers of the Gospel who take public stands. We should not be surprised, for Jesus told us that things like this would occur.

CHAPTER FIVE

What is the purpose of New Testament deacons?

Two Points if you answered: the purpose of New Testament deacons is to glorify God! We can, of course expand the meaning to specifically include: to glorify God by serving the Church. Or even by saying: the purpose of New Testament deacons is to serve the Church by ministering to the widows and by protecting the Pastor's study and prayer time, thus pleasing and glorifying God (bonus points for the expanded definition).

Here is another key question! If we take Acts 6 in the most literal meaning then we can see deacons have a very specific job description: one, to maintain an unreproachable feeding program for widows; and two, protect the time the apostles have set aside for prayer and study. If we also consider the two deacons, we know the most about, Stephen and Philip, then we would add street preaching and witnessing for the Kingdom plus a willingness to be used of God even unto death. This is much more than most wives of deacons and Pastor's wives have signed up for. Nevertheless, the Scripture is what the Scripture is!

Working with Pastors and deacons has led me to speak to some wives of deacons and Pastors. The most common complaint of Pastor wives and deacon wives is this: "I did not sign up for this!" Of course, most deacons are married before they become deacons. And many if not most Ministers accepted the call to minister early in their Christian walk. This is true in the life of this author. Here is another two cents worth of advice, worth just about that much. I strongly believe if a candidate for the office of Pastor or deacon is married or engaged then the wife should also be a part of the interview process. And she should be questioned as well. Way too often the process of interviewing Candidates for ministerial positions is too lax. When Churches license a person to Preach, the licensing Church takes on the responsibility of ensuring the person doing the preaching is well grounded and a representative of the licensing Church and the kingdom of God. When a Church ordains a minister, they also link themselves to the one they ordain. These processes should be done with at least as much reverence as when we share in the Lord's Supper and share together in Baptism. These proceedings should be held in a manner that reflects the gravity of what is being done.[61]

When believers enter the Christian faith, we claim Christ Jesus as our Savior, but also claim Him as our example. Jesus promised that suffering would come to the believer. Christians accept the whole Jesus package. Sold out for Jesus is an old phrase that has been lost to our most recent Church language. But this is precisely what deacons are called to be: sold out for Jesus!

In the nations that regularly persecute Christians, believers there would understand the ramifications of the phrase: "Sold out for Jesus"! Homes, livelihoods, wealth, wife, children, and torture await the believer in many places in today's world. These persecuting countries are only a few hours away by jet. The Voice of the Martyrs and the Persecuted Church are excellent organizations that often assist the wives and families of men of God who have been arrested or executed for their faith. Both groups are worthy of support to carry on this important work. The early Church suffered in a similar fashion to many Churches in Syria, India, and Indonesia. In this nation, are we moving in that direction? Many believe so, including this author. Let us pray that we will be able to maintain our witness in the coming troubling times ahead.

---

61   Musings of the Author.

World War II is known for the Jewish Holocaust. Fewer knew/know that many Christians were also persecuted and were also interred and/ or sent to work camps. During the time of Hitler's massive buildup of the German military machine, some problems Pastors were inducted into the German Army, separating them from their congregations and effectively silencing their voices in the public square. In the days leading up to WWII Christian Pastors were arrested if they were organizing and speaking out against Nazism and/or Hitler. One, such man was Dietrich Bonhoeffer. Here is a brief biographical sketch of Pastor Bonhoeffer. The author strongly recommends reading Pastor Bonhoeffer's biography.

The Life and Death of a Modern Martyr

> Born into privilege, Dietrich Bonhoeffer was headed toward a brilliant career as a theologian. Then he came to see life "from the perspective of those who suffer", in Nazi Germany, that cost him his life.[62]

One of the last direct orders Hitler gave was to order the execution of Pastor Bonhoeffer. When the guards came for him, they addressed him as Pastor. He forgave them for what they had been ordered to do – then his life ended. Pastor Bonhoeffer is an example to all men of God who face death in the cause of Christ Jesus. Today in our world many other Pastors and deacons have followed the way of other great men, who served God and faithfully, willingly marched to their deaths. Surely men like these died and awoke embraced by the arms of Jesus. These are heroes of the Faithful. Already in many parts of the world men and women of God are suffering and dying for Christ Jesus. Let us never forget to pray for those that face persecution daily.

History has confirmed the Nazi pattern of persecution. Historically the pattern is to arrest, imprison, torture, execute and confiscate the wealth

---

[62] Christian History Magazine-Issue 32: Dietrich Bonhoeffer: Theologian in Nazi Germany (Carol Stream, IL: Christianity Today, 1991,

of believers, thus leaving their families destitute as a sign for others who would dare preach the Gospel. Jesus, speaking of HIS death said the following:

> NKJV John 15: 18 **"If the world hates you, you know that it hated Me before** *it hated* **you.**
>
> [19] **If you were of the world, the world would love its own. Yet because you are not of the world, but I chose you out of the world, therefore the world hates you.** [20] **Remember the word that I said to you, 'A servant is not greater than his master.' If they persecuted Me, they will also persecute you.**

Persecution is part of our Spiritual DNA. The Church suffers in most of the nations of the world; why is the United States spared? Is it possible that a United States persecution is on the horizon? During Covid 19, in 2020, many American Churches were silenced and those that remained open were threatened and a few Pastors were arrested and fined, though these arrests and fines were largely overturned.

> NKJV Matthew 26: 31 **Then Jesus said to them, "All of you will be made to stumble because of Me this night, for it is written: 'I will strike the Shepherd, And the sheep of the flock will be scattered.'**

Jesus is quoting the prophet Zechariah 13: 7 who prophesied saying:

> NKJV **"Awake, O sword, against My Shepherd, Against the Man who is My Companion,"**
>
> **Says the Lord of hosts. "Strike the Shepherd, And the sheep will be scattered;**
>
> **Then I will turn My hand against the little ones.**

Sweet Jesus how precious are the little one to YOU. Again, we turn to Jesus' own words:

NKJV Matthew 18: 6 "**Whoever causes one of these little ones who believe in Me to sin, it would be better for him if a millstone were hung around his neck, and he were drowned in the depth of the sea.**

And within the same passage, Jesus returns to the phrase, "little ones".

NKJV Matthew 18: 10 "**Take heed that you do not despise one of these little ones, for I say to you that in heaven their angels always see the face of My Father who is in heaven.**

Who can imagine what kind of judgment of God, the Almighty, will bring to bear on those that harm the little ones of God? In today's world Christian girls are being kidnaped, raped, and sold into forced marriages. This was happening in the recently formed Islamic State instituted by radical Muslims (this state was targeted, destroyed, or driven underground by a coalition led by President Trump's Administration). And this continues to happen in some places in Northern Africa. What boundary does a wicked and evil man have except the hand of God? What demonic forces are at work in our world? In a world such as this the Church desperately needs little "d" deacons. If history is any judge, persecution will come first for the Pastor, then the Church will be driven underground. When this happens, it will be little "d" deacons who will be needed to minister to the Church in the midst of persecution. Deacons must be men of courage and stout of heart to continue in such moments.

The wickedness of man knows no boundaries. Unregenerate men and unregenerate nations have proved repeatedly the ability to invent more and more weapons of destruction and inventions of the cruelest torture. This is the heritage of sinful men: to persecute believers and the historic Chosen People of God (Jews). This seems to spur the creation of horrible demonic inventions designed for the sole purpose of implementing the cruelest of tortures. We can see in the radical Muslims that crucifixion is returning as a method of torturing believers, as are mass executions by beheading.

China has taken up the historic patterns of persecution, as have radical Muslims. This was also the pattern of Nazi Germany. Will this pattern continue to repeat itself? Only God knows, but it does seem likely. Will this pattern be repeated in the United States? If this pattern does repeat itself, then deacons will be left to lead the Church in its pastoral ministries. Pastors need to be involved and actively discipling their deacons and these deacons need to be actively discipling potential deacons. Is persecution coming, will the United States escape the persecution of the Church? If so, what Scripture supports this belief? The answer is **NONE!**

The first century Church suffered intense persecution. Read about the Seven Churches of Revelation and see how extensive persecutions were. The Church was called to be faithful even unto death. This is an early theme in Revelation. **Another purpose of the NT deacon is to stand with the Church amid persecution even unto death**. The Church is expected and commanded to endure. God's people are to be witnesses even unto death. Of course, these are hard sayings. The reality is many believers are suffering horrific attacks, even as this is being written. Persecution directed against Christians is on the rise around the World. The United Nations turns a blind eye, as do most of the Western Nations. Historic Mission sending nations are silent and deaf to the pleas of suffering Christians. The Nazi pattern is repeating itself. Governments are becoming increasingly hostile to the Church.

IN CONCLUSION

Deacons are increasingly called to stand with the Church amid increasing persecution. This is evident in the Middle East, The Far East, including China and North Korea (imagine being a deacon in North Korea, in an underground Church). Nazis came for Pastors who spoke against Hitler and his diabolical plans. Hitler persecuted Pastors who stood up for the Jews. Deacons were the ministers that were left at the local Church and they ministered to their people!

Additionally, deacons are to support their Pastor, specifically to protect the Pastor's time for study and prayer. Deacons, also, are to specifically care for widows and by extension the children of widows. Many women in our Churches are spiritual widows meaning that their husbands are lost or hostile to the Church and/or Jesus. In instances like this, deacon wives can and should play a more important role. Domestic violence is also on the rise; likely this will continue, as more husbands who are hostile to the Gospel will continue to make life difficult for their wives.

Most importantly, deacons are to be students of God's word, men of prayer, but also men of action. They need to be problem solvers just like the first seven deacons.

As persecutions continue for believers and as the United States moves toward paganism and atheistic policies, the United States Government will become increasingly hostile to believers and Jews. Deacons will be needed to stand in the gap.

> NKJV Ezekiel 22:29**The people of the land have used oppressions, committed robbery, and mistreated the poor and needy; and they wrongfully oppress the stranger.**

> **30 So I sought for a man among them who would make a wall, and stand in the gap before Me on behalf of the land, that I should not destroy it; but I found no one.**

> **31Therefore I have poured out My indignation on them; I have consumed them with the fire of My wrath; and I have recompensed their deeds on their own heads," says the Lord GOD.**

Ezekiel 22 speaks of a time when God looks for a man to stand in the gap but finds no one willing to stand for God. Jesus will one day call us home but until that day Pastors and little "d" deacons **MUST STAND IN THE GAP.** God's people need leaders filled with the zeal of God, passion, character, courage, and the confidence of the indwelling of the Holy Spirit of God. **Will the last days of the Church find people willing to stand in the GAP for God?** Who will stand and who will be found faithful?

CHAPTER SIX

Qualifications for Deacons

Prior to turning our attention to the qualifications of deacons; there are other passages of Scripture that speak about deacons; only 1 Timothy speaks directly to the qualifications of deacons. Additional passages enlighten us *about* deacons but only 1 Timothy speaks specifically *to* deacons. There are other verses we will examine first, including 1 Timothy 3: 8 that will provide an introduction to our study of the qualification of a deacon.

> NKJV Philippians 1:1 **Paul and Timothy, bondservants of Jesus Christ, To all the saints in Christ Jesus who are in Philippi, with the bishops (overseers) and deacons**

The writer of Philippians specifically mentioned deacons! There must have been outstanding deacons in Philippi too. Perhaps it is possible that Stephen and Philip were not as unique as many believe, but these two, we know a great deal about: street preaching and public witnessing was initiated by these two men. Times were tough for the early Church. But one thing was certain, deacons in Philippi had been noticed by the writer of Philippians and demonstrate that deacons played a role in the early Church that often suffered state sponsored persecution. The Book of Philippians is worthy of study demonstrating the loving generosity of this early Church (even while suffering) and was uniquely special to the apostle Paul. Plus, with a basic reading of Philippians the reader can see that the persecution of the Church was an ever-present concern of the early Church, just like the Church in Jerusalem. Christian persecution has always been an ever-present possibility. It is obvious to anyone paying any attention to the current news to see how the Church is persecuted.

One more passage of Scripture should be mentioned: In this instance two translations will be shared together for clarity:

> NKJV Romans 16:1 **I commend to you Phoebe our sister, who is a servant (_deacon_** _(added by author for comparison)_**) of the church in Cenchrea, ²that you may receive her in the Lord in a manner worthy of the saints and assist her in <u>whatever business</u> she has need of you; for indeed she has been a helper of many and of myself also.**

Compare the above translation with the following:

> Revised Standard Version Romans 16:1 **I commend to you our sister Phoebe, a <u>deaconess</u> of the church at Cenchre-ae, ²that you may receive her in the Lord as befits the saints, and help her in <u>whatever she may require</u> from you, for she has been a helper of many and of myself as well.**[63]

This is the only mention of Phoebe in the New Testament. Surely, she must have been highly regarded by the apostle Paul and by her local Church. Perhaps she was the wife of a deacon. Others suggest[64] she was

---

63   _The Revised Standard Version_ (Oak Harbor, WA: Logos Research Systems, Inc., 1971), Ro 16:1–2.

64   Jack Cottrell, _Romans_, vol. 2, The College Press NIV Commentary (Joplin, MO: College Press Pub. Co., 1996), Ro 16:1. What does Paul mean when he calls Phoebe a _servant_ of the church in Cenchrea? This is a matter of considerable controversy. Paul uses the Greek word διάκονος (_diakonos_), a word which is masculine in form but was used for both men and women. Its basic connotation is "servant, helper, one who carries out the will or purpose of another, one who ministers to the needs of others." The _NT_ usually uses it in this generic sense for Christian workers (and others). In this case the English word "servant" is most appropriate.

But on at least three occasions (Phil 1:1; 1 Tim 3:8, 12) this word seems to be used for a more or less "official" role of service in the church—"official" in the sense that the individual is selected and appointed by the local congregation

a servant in the sense of assisting the apostle Paul and others during a sickness or some other issue that may have happened. Others suggest[65] a more formal role as a deaconess.

This is what we know: Phoebe was considered as a servant by Paul and is now on a journey to Rome representing her Church well. A woman traveling alone would be unusual in her day and it seems logical that the apostle wrote this glowing recommendation for Phoebe to be used during her travels relying on the generosity of local Churches along the way. With such a recommendation she would have been granted lodging and other assistance by the local Churches. Was Phoebe a deaconess? Perhaps, but the scholars are not in full agreement. For this reason, we will not spend time on the possibility of female deacons. Clearly, she was held in high esteem by Paul and by her Church. But it is not clear if she was on Church business or some private business. Had it been

---

to be responsible for a specific task within or on behalf of that congregation. In this latter case the English word "deacon" is used. AND. The English word "minister" should be avoided in translations, since it has a limited modern cultural connotation with no real parallel in the *NT*. "Ministry" as a translation for the related word *diakonia* is appropriate, though, since its connotations can be more general.

[65] H. D. M. Spence-Jones, ed., *The Pulpit Commentary: Romans*, The Pulpit Commentary (London; New York: Funk & Wagnalls Company, 1909), 454. Phæbe was probably the bearer of the Epistle. She appears to have had business, perhaps of a legal kind, that took her to Rome; and St. Paul took advantage of her going to send the letter by her, desiring also to enlist the aid of her fellow-Christians at Rome in furtherance of her business, whatever it might be. Her having business at Rome, and her having been "a succorer of many," suggests the idea of her being a lady of means. Her designation as διάκονος of the Church at Cenchrea probably implies that she held an office there corresponding to that of *deaconess*, though there is no reason to suppose the distinguishing term διακόνισσα to have been as yet in use. Her function, and that of others (as perhaps of Tryphena and Tryphosa, mentioned in ver. 12 as "labouring much in the Lord"), might be to minister to the sick and poor, and to fulfil such charitable offices as women could best discharge. Cf. 1 Tim. 3:11, where γυναῖκας, mentioned in the midst of directions as to the qualifications of *men* for the office of deacons, probably denotes *women* who fulfilled similar duties.

clear that she was on Church business then the evidence would support her identity as a **deaconess**!

Is it possible that Phoebe was used as a secret agent used to smuggle or secretly carry Paul's letters to Rome? Although there is **NO evidence** to support this theory, it does seem plausible. And would answer a few of the controversial aspects of this passage of Scripture. It would also explain Paul's introduction letter to the Church in Rome. In the Roman male-dominated world that Phoebe lived, a woman carrying Paul's letter would not likely be suspected as a Christian smuggler. Was Phoebe the first Bible smuggler, maybe? Studying Scripture allows the student to discover wonderful possibilities from the Bible that a casual reader might miss.

Now we come to the qualifications of a deacon.

Qualifications are not suggestions—they are THE qualifications; this is not a fine line but an important distinction. An individual desiring to become a deacon **must be qualified** or the Church will suffer for it. Many Churches use their deacons in roles that are not specifically Biblical; for instance, they are used in administrative roles. Often this is codified in the Church Covenant and/or the Churches Bylaws. Deacons perform their best when they are allowed to be little "d" deacons. The qualifications are as follows: NKJV 1 Timothy 3: 8 and following,

> [8]**Likewise deacons** *must be* **reverent,**
> > **not double-tongued,**
> > **not given to much wine,**
> > **not greedy for money,**
> [9]**holding the mystery of the faith with a pure conscience.**
> [10]**But let these also first be tested;**
> > **then let them serve as deacons, being** *found* **blameless.**
> [11] **Likewise,** *their* **wives** *must be* **reverent,**
> > **not slanderers,**
> > **temperate,**
> > **faithful in all things.**

¹²**Let deacons be the husbands of one wife,**
ruling *their* **children**
and their own houses well.
¹³**For those who have served well as deacons obtain for themselves**
a good standing and great boldness in the faith which is in Christ
Jesus.

Some see an evolution of deacons from Acts to 1 Timothy: from a position of Christian service to a leadership position (though in lesser rank than Pastors/Bishops). To argue such a position, would seem to take away from Luke's account about Stephen and Philip. It seems **impossible to suggest that Philip and Stephen were not leaders**. It seems much more likely that 1 Timothy's list of qualifications is more of a reflection on the expansion of the Church throughout the Roman Empire. As the Church grew, the distance between the Church and the Apostles became greater. The only choice the apostles had was to write the Gospels and send letters to the ever-growing Church. The geographically spreading Church made it no longer possible for the Apostles to personally supervise all the local Churches. This distance in time and geography increased the need for the written Word of God. As the apostles suffered martyrdom and arrest like the apostle John, their letters and writings became more crucial. We have the qualifications of deacons for this reason. **Praise God that we have a Bible that we can rely on as trustworthy, in all things pertaining to faith and practice. Thank God we have qualifications for both Pastors and deacons.**

The apostle Paul, in writing to Timothy, preserves for us the qualification of deacons. Hopefully, we remember discussing that the word "deacon" and "servant" are interchangeable. Careful consideration should be paid to the following:

> The term *deacon* comes from the Greek word *diakonos*, meaning a helper or a servant, and is sometimes translated "minister." The apostle Paul frequently uses this term to describe himself

and his co-workers (see, for example, 1 Cor 3:5; 2 Cor 3:6; Rom 16:1; Col 1:23; 4:7).[66]

There is nothing wrong with being a servant following the Biblical role that Jesus instituted. Sometimes Big " D" deacon have said: "I am nobodies' servant."[67] When we serve, we do as Jesus did both as an example in HIS earthly ministry and in HIS death and resurrection – HE is our Suffering Servant.[68] Paul uses servant to describe himself,

---

[66]   Daniel C. Arichea and Howard Hatton, *A Handbook on Paul's Letters to Timothy and to Titus*, UBS Handbook Series (New York: United Bible Societies, 1995), 71–72.

[67]   I heard this in a Big "D" Deacons meeting at a Church in Tuscaloosa, Alabama. All but one was shocked, but he continued to be a deacon and several years later he still serves.

[68]   Suffering Servant Songs (42:1–4; 49:1–6; 50:4–9; 52:13–53:12; with expansions in 42:5–9; 49:7–13; 50:10–11). The identity of the Suffering Servant is uncertain (→ Servant of the Lord). Walter Dietrich, "Isaiah, Book of," *The Encyclopedia of Christianity* (Grand Rapids, MI; Leiden, Netherlands: Wm. B. Eerdmans; Brill, 1999–2003), 747. Additionally:

1.   He is elected by the Lord, anointed by the Spirit, and promised success in his endeavor (42:1, 4).
2.   Justice is a prime concern of his ministry (42:1, 4).
3.   His ministry has an international scope (42:1, 6).
4.   God predestined him to his calling (49:1).
5.   He is a gifted teacher (49:2).
6.   He experiences discouragement in his ministry (49:4).
7.   His ministry extends to the Gentiles (49:6).
8.   The Servant encounters strong opposition and resistance to his teaching, even of a physically violent nature (50:4–6).
9.   He is determined to finish what God called him to do (50:7).
10.   The Servant has humble origins with little outward prospects for success (53:1–2).
11.   He experiences suffering and affliction (53:3).
12.   The Servant accepts vicarious and substitutionary suffering on behalf of his people (53:4–6, 12).
13.   He is put to death after being condemned (53:7–9).
14.   Incredibly, he comes back to life and is exalted above all rulers (53:10–12; 52:13–15

Norman L. Geisler and Frank Turek, *I Don't Have Enough Faith to Be an Atheist* (Wheaton, IL: Crossway Books, 2004), 332–333.

fellow ministers, Church leaders and a variety of other Church members. It was also used of government officials. Deacons are servants and there is nothing wrong to be known as a servant of God. What better title is there than to be known as one of HIS servants?

The Apostle Paul sends this letter (1 Timothy) to Timothy, who is a young Pastor at The Church of Ephesus, which was also one of the Churches addressed in Revelation. Paul gives guidance to Timothy on many issues, including being faithful to the doctrines of the Church (**Do you know what the doctrines of the Church are?**). Paul encourages Timothy and speaks sound words of direction regarding men and women of the Church; then Paul in Chapter 3 focuses on emphasizing the qualifications of Overseers (Pastors) and deacons. And it is in these qualifications of deacons we shall focus.

NKJV 1 Timothy 3: 8 and following

> **⁸Likewise deacons *must be* reverent,**
> > **not double-tongued,**
> > **not given to much wine,**
> > **not greedy for money,**
> **⁹holding the mystery of the faith with a pure conscience.**
> **¹⁰But let these also first be tested;**
> > **then let them serve as deacons, being *found* blameless.**
> **¹¹Likewise, *their* wives *must be* reverent,**
> > **not slanderers,**
> > **temperate,**
> > **faithful in all things.**
> **¹²Let deacons be the husbands of one wife,**
> > **ruling their children**
> > **and their own houses well.**
> **13 For those who have served well as deacons obtain for themselves a good standing and great boldness in the faith which is in Christ Jesus.**

Now back to Bible study. We will complete our introduction to 1 Timothy 3 by Looking at verse 13. Verse 13 is not a qualification as are the other verses. Verse 13 tells us what the individual earns as he ministers effectively.

We are saved by Grace. This is clear both in the Old Testament and the New. Presumably, deacons have already experienced GOD'S SAVING GRACE and have demonstrated a clear testimony of Jesus Christ. These men who have served well as deacons obtain for themselves a good standing. This is an interesting way to phrase this. They did not obtain for the Church or for the Kingdom but for themselves. The idea here is like Jesus' parable of the Good Steward (Servant). The phrase, "a good standing" is the literal translation but in this case, it does not present the whole story. A better translation, capturing the full meaning, might look like the following: "are highly esteemed by their fellow Christians and by God."[69] This captures the full intent of the apostle Paul and reminds us that the deacon ministry was primarily directed to those within the community of Christ! Christian believers need ministry too. Especially during our current Covid scare. This is an opportunity for deacons to shine. The primary focus of the original seven deacons was directed at the care of widows. Deacons could be seizing on the opportunity to deliver food and transport others to the store or doctor's offices. Little "d" deacons will minister to those within the Church during this difficult time. And if not then the heart of the deacons in any given Church will be found out.

These early deacons may have already "obtained a good standing" and demonstrated "great boldness in the faith". This is not a qualification; this is the result of serving as a deacon. Churches sometimes select deacons because they are the only men in a Church or because the constitution of the Church demands that you have seven deacons. Being a good ol'boy or being well liked or well connected to key Church members is not a good reason to select someone as a deacon. Therefore, allowing the Scripture to speak for itself in the matter of choosing deacons is key to having EXCELLENT deacons instead of having

---

[69] Daniel C. Arichea and Howard Hatton, *A Handbook on Paul's Letters to Timothy and to Titus*, UBS Handbook Series (New York: United Bible Societies, 1995), 77.

men serving as figureheads or placeholders or rewarding a man with a title just because he is there. Qualifications for a deacon candidate is the **minimum standard**. Just being a mature man is not a qualification enough; nor does just being the last man standing qualify him for deacon ministry. Fulfilling the qualifications is essential to be faithful to the word of God in this ministry. No shortcuts are allowed. Returning to verse 13:

> **[13]For those who have served well as deacons obtain for themselves <u>a good standing</u> and <u>great boldness</u> in the faith which is in Christ Jesus.**

Perhaps a better translation, capturing the full meaning, could look like the following: "are highly esteemed by their fellow Christians and by God."[70] This captures the full intent of the apostle Paul. We are looking at verse 13 first, because this verse establishes what a little "d" deacon looks like as he serves **the body of Christ** and the **Kingdom**. A deacon who has served well has **a good standing** and **great boldness** in the faith. What is the full meaning of these two phrases?

> **"a good standing"**: This phrase is somewhat ambiguous. "Does the mention of an *excellent standing and great assurance* speak to the deacon's being respected in the eyes of God, the eyes of the church, or the eyes of the community? It could be all three".[71] This seems to fit with the natural, simple reading. One word of caution; the phrase **"obtain for themselves a good standing"** "does not necessarily refer to a higher leadership position (i.e., pastor), but possibly respect within their community, which allows them to boldly share the gospel.[72]" Naturally, this makes

---

70 Daniel C. Arichea and Howard Hatton, *A Handbook on Paul's Letters to Timothy and to Titus*, UBS Handbook Series (New York: United Bible Societies, 1995), 77.

71 Doug Redford, *The New Testament Church: Acts-Revelation*, vol. 2, Standard Reference Library: New Testament (Cincinnati, OH: Standard Pub., 2007), 238.

72 Robert James Utley, *Paul's Fourth Missionary Journey: I Timothy, Titus, II Timothy*, vol. Volume 9, Study Guide Commentary Series (Marshall, Texas:

sense, for the deacon has met the qualifications and been obedient/faithful in the performing of his duties. Then it follows and makes sense that God, the Church, and the community see in this man godly attributes. Look again at Acts 6:

NKJV Acts 6: 6-7 **whom they set before <u>the apostles</u>; and when they had <u>prayed, they laid hands on them</u>. ⁷<u>Then the word of God spread</u>, and the <u>number</u> of the disciples <u>multiplied</u> greatly in Jerusalem, and a great <u>many</u> of the <u>priests were obedient to the faith</u>.**

The above Scripture is underscored and in bold type for emphasis to illustrate the following: the establishment and the good work of the earliest deacons and **BANG, POW, BOOM,** explosive growth occurred. Good works affect successful evangelism outreach. When the Church is doing great things then the Holy Spirit has something to brag about. This is further illustrated by Philip's and Stephen's actions highlighted in the Book of Acts.

Stephen: The first martyr of the Church, gave an amazing testimony in which he saw: "the Kingdom of Heaven open and Jesus" (Acts 7: 55-56). We also see of other exploits of Stephen, Acts 6: 8 "And Stephen, full of faith and power, did great wonders and signs among the people." Stephen, a little "d" deacon was involved in the supernatural acts of God.

Philip: Philip, also one of the original Seven little "d" deacons also did wonders and signs (Acts 8: 4 and following). Philip also preached as Jesus did in Samaria, the land of the unclean 1st cousins of the Jews.

Philip drew crowds in Samaria because of his preaching and healing ministry. The Greek indicates that he kept on doing miracles while the crowds continued to listen and watch him. The people gave Philip

---

Bible Lessons International, 2000), 48.

their undivided attention; through the preaching of the gospel and the evidence of divine miracles, they came to faith in Christ.

The result of the preaching ministry was the Second Revival of Samaria, following on the heels of the Revival started by Jesus with one woman at a well. Being used of God to Preach Jesus in Samaria Philip was plucked from this fruitful ministry and sent to one lonely man[73] in a distant desert. Look at how great God's concern is for even a single individual. Philip is taken from a multitude to meet with an Ethiopian Eunuch who is returning home. In this meeting God used Philip to begin a work in Africa. One cannot help but think how similar Jesus' parable (Luke 15: 14) about the one lost sheep and Philip's lost Ethiopian.

Philip was also known for having four daughters who prophesied. Not a great deal is known about his daughters within Scripture. Outside of Scripture we have some excellent sources regarding these women.

> **"had four virgin daughters...prophetesses"** We need to rethink our position on women in leadership positions (cf. Joel 2:28–32; Acts 2:16–21) in the church based on all of New Testament evidence. See Special Topic: Women in the Bible at 2:17. The issue is ambiguous. Church tradition says that they moved to Asia Minor (Phrygia) and that his daughters lived long and served God to a very old age. We learn this tradition from Eusebius, who quotes from both Polycrates and Papias (compare *Eccl. Hist.* 3:31:2–5).[74]

---

[73] Having established the mission to the Samaritans, Philip then became involved in an even more far-reaching missionary breakthrough, as he was led to witness to an Ethiopian. Indeed, Philip's witness to the eunuch may be considered the first conversion of a Gentile and in many ways parallels the story of Cornelius in chapter 10. John B. Polhill, vol. 26, *Acts*, The New American Commentary (Nashville: Broadman & Holman Publishers, 1995), 222

[74] Robert James Utley, vol. Volume 3B, *Luke the Historian: The Book of Acts*, Study Guide Commentary Series (Marshall, TX: Bible Lessons International, 2003), 240.

This information does not change our understanding of Scripture or of our Faith and Practice. However, we see that Philip's family was special and his daughters were spectacular servants too. One of the qualifications of deacons is that they ruled their house well. The evidence of scripture proves that Philip raised his daughters well.

Clearly, both Philip and Stephen were on **FIRE** for the Gospel (as were Philip's daughters) just as were the apostles during Pentecost. Are these two little "d" deacons unique? The emphasis that Luke, the writer of Acts, places on them, plus the language he uses suggests that they were not unique! They were filled with the Holy Spirit of God. Consider Mr. Litfin's comments regarding Acts 3: 13:

> Though the position of deacon seems by worldly standards to be menial and unattractive, **to close followers of Jesus Christ** it looks quite different (cf. John 13:11–17; Mark 10:42–45). Those who fulfill their servant roles faithfully **gain** two things: first, **an excellent standing** before fellow Christians who understand and appreciate the beauty of humble, selfless, Christlike service; and second, **great assurance** (*parrēsian*, "confidence, boldness") **in their faith in Christ Jesus**. Humble service, which lacks all the rewards the world deems important, becomes a true test of one's motives. Here one discovers for himself whether or not his efforts are truly prompted by a Christlike spirit of selfless service. When a deacon has indeed "served well" his ministry builds confidence in the sincerity of his own faith in Christ and of his unhypocritical approach to God (cf. Eph. 3:12; Heb. 10:19).[75]

Mr. Litfin's comments are right on target! Active Christian service should ignite and fire up our mission to witness for Jesus. The fire of the Holy Spirit moves the believer into service and godly service excites

---

[75] A. D. Litfin, "1 Timothy," in *The Bible Knowledge Commentary: An Exposition of the Scriptures*, ed. Walvoord and Zuck, vol. 2 (Wheaton, IL: Victor Books, 85), 738.

the believer to proclaim the Gospel to desperate people. Godly service moves the servant ever closer to being more and more like Jesus.

Continuing to examine phrases of the deacon qualifications:

"**Great Boldness**"; this phrase is not nearly so ambiguous as our previous phrase "**good standing**"! For instance: **Boldness** (παρρησίαν); is quite common in the New Testament (comp. Acts 4:13, 29, 31; Eph. 6:19; Phil. 1:20, etc.), where it is especially applied to boldness in preaching the gospel of Christ. This seems to imply that St. Paul contemplated preaching as a part of the deacon's work. We know that Philip the deacon and Stephen the deacon "preached".[76] In the contemporary Church most believe that preaching is reserved for those called to do so. Clearly Stephen and Philip preached the Word of God to great effect, blessed by Spiritual fruit.

The phrase "**Great Boldness**" as seen in 1 Timothy 3: 13 led to a number of little "d" deacon firsts: the first martyr was a deacon – Stephen. The first gentile was won to Christ by a deacon – Philip, who started international missions. The first evangelist was a deacon. Deacons led out and helped to establish Churches outside of Jerusalem. These were not timid men. These were courageous men facing a world that looked at Christianity as a cult. And yet, they bravely faced opposition, and in Stephen's case, died because of the tremendous evil directed at early Christians. We cannot help but marvel at the zeal of Stephen and Philip. Luke's wording (in Acts) inspires us to look at Philip and Stephen and be inspired at their zeal and boldness. Verse 13 tells us that results are expected of little "d" deacons. Philip and Stephen were the ideal deacons, for Luke. The qualifications of deacons are the minimum standard for a deacon. The goal is to be more than the qualifications. The goal is to be a great little "d" deacon. Anything less is to tarnish the great heritage that belongs to deacons.

---

[76] H. D. M. Spence-Jones, ed., _1 Timothy_, The Pulpit Commentary (London; New York: Funk & Wagnalls Company, 1909), 54.

INTRODUCTION CONCLUSION: Qualifications are the minimum standard. The Church needs men that exceed the minimum standard. We have minimum standards for driving: you must be 16 years old, you must have automobile insurance, you must pass a written test, you must pass a driving test, you must pass an eye exam and you must have someone willing to give you the keys to their car. As a driver on the public streets, you want the other drivers to have achieved more than the minimum passing grades on the written and driving tests. Although highway driving seems to prove that many only have the minimum of skills needed to drive safely, driving the city streets prove that many more should have more than the minimum grade on the eye exam. Our preference is to have all new drivers exceed the minimum standards. We all get the idea, the Church should want men who exceed the minimum standards, like a Stephen and a Philip.

Deacon qualifications, as outlined in 1 Timothy 3, are more stringent than one might at first believe. In the next section we will delve into the qualifications of deacons as sent to Timothy from the apostle Paul.

QUALIFICATIONS OF DEACONS:

NKJV 1 Timothy 3: 8 and following

> [8]**Likewise deacons** *must be* **reverent,**
> **not double-tongued,**
> **not given to much wine,**
> **not greedy for money,**
> [9]**holding the mystery of the faith with a pure conscience.**
> **10But let these also first be tested;**
> **then let them serve as deacons, being** *found* **blameless.**
> [11]**Likewise,** *their* **wives** *must be* **reverent,**
> **not slanderers,**
> **temperate,**
> **faithful in all things.**
> [12]**Let deacons be the husbands of one wife,**
> **ruling** *their* **children**

and their own houses well.

Five verses that define the beginnings of an ancient deacon ministry dating back to the early days of the Church. History matters and as far as Scripture is concerned, it is the History of the Ancient Church! And deacons carry on a proud ancient tradition—a ministry rooted in ancient Scripture and tied to the specific needs of the Church and their Pastors. Our understanding of these five verses will forever define the individual deacon. In this second section of little "d" deacon qualifications we will do an in-depth study into these words of Paul to his student: young Pastor Timothy, as Timothy seeks to establish a New Testament Church.

> **⁸Likewise deacons *must be* reverent,**
> **not double-tongued,**
> **not given to much wine,**
> **not greedy for money,**

Let our prayer be: Heavenly Father, as we search the Scriptures, let us endeavor to serve the Church and build your Kingdom, In Jesus name. This kind of prayer should be on the lips of every voting member when voting for a deacon.

Verse 8: In verse 8 we have one "must BE" and three "must not BE's". As we enter the Biblical qualifications of deacons let us be ever mindful of the importance of following God's Word.

Likewise

Likewise, is our first word as we study deacon qualifications. Previously Paul discussed the qualifications of Bishops/Pastors. Likewise links the two passages together. Reading the passage concerning Bishops/Pastors along with deacon qualifications, one cannot help but notice how similar both passages are. The apostle Paul, using similar language, illustrates the gravity of both positions: Bishops/Pastors and deacons.[77] Both are worthy services.

---

[77] Daniel C. Arichea and Howard Hatton, *A Handbook on Paul's Letters to Timothy and to Titus*, UBS Handbook Series (New York: United Bible Societies, 1995), 72.

deacons *must be* reverent

Here we begin with the meat and potatoes of this passage. Reverent has been translated in several ways: grave, serious and the ESV has dignified. Using a common thesaurus provide more choices: Respectful, Worshipful, Awed and Humble. J Vernon McGee, famous for his radio program *Through the Bible*, prefers the word, "Grave"—he should be a man of dignity.[78] No one suggests that a deacon should be so serious that he looks like a mortician looking for his next body. But he should be serious-minded of the things of God's Kingdom and the care of God's people. His feet should be planted in both Worlds. He needs to be a man rooted in Scripture practice and knowledge. Certainly, a Bible student.

> . . . deacons must be *serious*. This is the same word used in (1 Timothy) 3:4 (there translated "respectful"). The term in fact includes a wide range of meanings: dignified, worthy of respect, having a good character (compare TE[79]V), high principled, honorable, "dignified" (RE[80]B), "respectable" (NJ[81]B).[82]

Clearly there is a lot here. A serious understanding of these qualifications is necessary to protect the Church and the reputation of the other deacons. It is best that deacons hold one another accountable, but this is often overlooked. This is of particular importance when the work of the deacon ministry is not fruitful. Being an effective deacon is also a burden for deacons, for deacons tend to be the face of the Church even more so than the Pastor. Imagine bring in a new deacon and discovering that he is not serious minded about the things of God.

---

[78] J. Vernon McGee, *Thru the Bible Commentary*, electronic ed., vol. 5 (Nashville: Thomas Nelson, 1997), 443.

[79] TEV Today's English Version

[80] REB Revised English Bible

[81] NJB New Jerusalem Bible

[82] Daniel C. Arichea and Howard Hatton, *A Handbook on Paul's Letters to Timothy and to Titus*, UBS Handbook Series (New York: United Bible Societies, 1995), 72.

(The author adding his two cents, again) As a young, newly licensed preacher, I was invited to Preach at a central Alabama Church. I arrived early enough to go to Sunday School and was ushered into a Sunday School Class of much older men. Later I learned this was the deacon's class. Each man took his turn and read their part of the Quarterly Sunday School Lesson. This was accomplished in about 20 minutes. A very brief generic prayer was said, and the talk immediately turned to Alabama Football. I witnessed nothing that led me to think that these men were serious-minded about the things of God's Kingdom. This encounter broke my heart.

The needs and duties of a deacon can be weighty. Every deacon needs to be able to carry his on weight and be an independent thinker as well as a self-starter.

Accordingly, deacons similarly (must be): (1) **Dignified:** See also Titus 2:2; cf. Phil. 4:8. For the noun see on 1 Tim. 2:2; Titus 2:7. This refers not only to their necessary decorum or propriety of manner and conduct but also to the fact that in their inner thoughts and attitudes they must be men of Spirit-wrought in gravity and respectability. Such serious-minded men were[83] Stephen and Philip.

The most mentioned deacons in Scripture are shining examples for deacons of any age. We have already spent time on Stephen and Philip. We can see by their examples that they were serious about the things of God and solving the practical needs of the Christian community. It is difficult if not impossible to choose which qualification is the most important. The apostle Paul was used of God to lay out these qualifications and each must be taken seriously to preserve the whole.

---

[83] W Hendriksen and S J. Kistemaker, _Exposition of the Pastoral Epistles_, vol. 4, New Testament Commentary (Grand Rapids: Baker Book House, 1953–2001), 130.

not double-tongued

Watching the 1950's Cowboy television shows or Western movies, any casual listener would hear the phrase: "White man speaks with forked tongue". This captures the meaning here.

NKJV James 5: 12 **But above all, my brethren, do not swear, either by heaven or by earth or with any other oath. But let your "Yes" be "Yes," and *your* "No," "No," lest you fall into judgment.**

This is an excellent motto for ministering deacons.

Be focused and thoughtful in our speech. Let us practice thinking before we speak. This is good advice; every thought in our head is not of divine origin. This includes young preacher boys too. The Biblical expectations for Pastors and deacons have many commonalities. As we see, James the apostle has a lot of practical suggestions for anyone in Church Service.

This is also the first of three prohibitions. On the battlefield, commanders need trustworthy information and intelligence reports of the enemy numbers and movement. Listening and observing military commanders during combat operations reveals that no commander ever feels he has enough information. Poor commanders wait and are hesitant to act and some act too brashly. A good commander understands when he must act. The same traits exist in soldiers too. Pastors need information just like commanders. Therefore, accuracy and truthfulness are key just like in the Army. Deacons need to be ethically free of entanglements and divided loyalty. They need to able to be trusted by their Pastors and the Church. When the office of the Pastor and his relationship with deacons are Biblically based, few closer relationships can exist. Reading the book of Acts, we have examples of the benefits of the local Pastor working closely with the deacons of the same local Church.

He does not say one thing to one person and something different to another. He does not "talk out of both sides of his mouth." He does not *say* one thing and *know* another, like: *Gehazi* (2

Kings 5:19–27) or *Sanballet and Geshem* (Neh. 6:2) or *Ananias and Sapphira*[84]

Every word out of a deacon's mouth must be truthful. All the qualifications point out the importance of a great character of high moral standards. If a deacon is asked a question, he should not pretend ignorance, he should answer truthfully, and if he needs to protect a confidence let him remain silent.

James McGowin (author's father) was a deacon and only recently passed away. He once confessed that of all the things he missed from his youth, he missed running the most. At his funeral, his eldest son pictured him running to Jesus; this has been his comfort. As a deacon, James McGowin tried to always say yes to his Pastor, in big or little things. The Church was small, and James was the only adult male so most of the weight of ministry fell on his shoulders. While he was still able to have a garden, James provided food for many elder women of the Church. It was said at his funeral "you could always count on a fresh tomato from James". He saw many Pastors come and go but he remained, serving his Church and ministering to those in the Kingdom. Deacons like James are a rare treasure.

Deacons need to be known as truth tellers both within and without the Church walls. They need to be faithful to telling the truth in business and be known for their honesty. Remember Acts 6: 6b-7.

> **. . . when they had prayed, they laid hands on them (deacons).**
> Acts 6: 7 **Then the word of God spread, and the number of the disciples multiplied greatly in Jerusalem, and a great many of the priests were obedient to the faith.**[85]

---

84 W Hendriksen and S J. Kistemaker, *Exposition of the Pastoral Epistles*, vol. 4, New Testament Commentary (Grand Rapids: Baker Book House, 1953–2001), 131.

85 *The New King James Version* (Nashville: Thomas Nelson, 1982), Ac 6:6–7.

How the local Church deacons are known or not known speaks volumes about the Church. It is impossible to invent a good reputation and keep it. Lawyers and Used Car Salesman have a terrible reputation. largely due to people's misfortunes with isolated Lawyers and Car Salesman. Imagine if your Church's deacons had the reputation of a Used Car Salesman. Being known for speaking the truth translates well to being able to share the Gospel. Why should anyone pay attention to a Church's deacon if that deacon just sold them a car that has more in common with a lemon than it does with worthwhile transportation? Trust matters and once lost is almost impossible to regain.

Another way of looking at **"not double tonged"** is double talking, generally defined as hypocritical or insincere speech. Putting people off or delaying in talking with them makes it difficult to be sincere when we finally do "get around to speaking to them". False sincerity is just another way to lie just as any false interest. Being truthful is the best policy. If you do not know, say so. Get back with them and give them the right answer. It is far better to delay an answer that to get it wrong.

Not given to much wine

It is important to be honest with Scripture. The Bible does not categorially reject drinking alcohol. Claims that Jesus drank only grape juice are wrong and silly and do not line up with Scripture. Scripture places limits on drinking: for example, it is not acceptable to be drunk.

> Lot's daughters made their father drunk (Gen. 19:32–5); David made Uriah drunk (2 Sam. 11:13); give the Rechabites wine to drink (Jer. 35:2–6); you made the Nazirites drink wine (Amos 2:12); woe to those who make others drunk to look at their nakedness (Hab. 2:15).[86]

These are just some of the examples of horrific sin linked to drunkenness. Drunkenness is a sin; no explanation is necessary. The author **is not**

---

[86] A. Colin Day, *Collins Thesaurus of the Bible* (Bellingham, WA: Logos Bible Software, 2009).

advocating that deacons can drink if they are not drunk. Individual Churches and denominations can put reasonable restrictions on their ministers. All communities are not the same just as all nations are not the same. **Avoiding alcohol is an excellent idea, for it separates us from the world in dramatic fashion**. In many office parties a non-drinker stands out, like a sore thumb, and has excellent opportunities to witness and to provide a service by driving people home. Abstaining from alcohol provides many opportunities to minister to others. And for most of us, avoiding all forms of alcohol is difficult as it is found in many medicines. Even Timothy is given some medical advice from the apostle Paul to take some wine for his stomach issues: NKJV 1 Timothy 5: 23. Alcoholism and drug addictions wreck families and lives. Why would a Christian family keep such things in the home? It is a risk we need not take. The number of Alcohol and Drug Dependent treatment facilities abound and are a large industry draining the pockets of families. **It is better to stay away from alcohol and illicit drugs**. This just makes sense. Scripture allows for the use of Alcohol (Beer, Wine, etc.). Likely, very few of us have escaped the harm and suffering that alcohol or illicit drugs can bring to many families. Drunk driving, drug dependency, alcoholism, there are countless ways these bring suffering to families. It is no wonder why the **Scriptures forbid drunkenness**. Again, to be fair with Scripture, Scripture does not forbid drinking. Abstaining from alcoholic beverages, including wine and beer, is a safe approach and the approach the author recommends. This provides a separation from the common public and demonstrates to the world that believers are both separate from the world while remaining in this world. Tattoos are popular in today's culture but there is a clear prohibition against tattoos as well. Tattoos are strictly forbidden, while drinking alcohol has many Biblical limitations. Consistency is important. Honesty with the Scripture is an important principle when examining the Bible.

23No longer drink only water but use a little wine for your stomach's sake and your frequent infirmities.

It seems that Timothy was abstaining from wine to keep himself pure, similar to the vow of a Nasserite: certainly, this is a good position to take as a Pastor or any minister. Pastors, deacons, and Churches do not need to give the media and the world free shots at believers. Abstaining from alcohol is a good policy.

> NKJV Numbers 6:1 **Then the Lord spoke to Moses, saying, ²"Speak to the children of Israel, and say to them: 'When either a man or woman consecrates an offering to take the vow of a Nazirite, to separate himself to the Lord, ³he shall separate himself from wine and *similar* drink; he shall drink neither vinegar made from wine nor vinegar made from *similar* drink; neither shall he drink any grape juice, nor eat fresh grapes or raisins. ⁴All the days of his separation he shall eat nothing that is produced by the grapevine, from seed to skin.**

These are just some of the requirements of a Nasserite Vow. Timothy took his appointment as Pastor very seriously. The minimum standard is that alcohol should not impair the dignity nor the judgement of a deacon. Drunkenness would disqualify someone from serving as a deacon or to continue to serve as a deacon. Many Churches categorially reject the use of alcohol for its ministers. **The author supports this position.**

Not greedy for money

Some phrases are hard to breakdown and explain. In this case that is not a problem. If you can recall a movie or a picture book about a short story written by Charles Dickens, entitled "The Christmas Carol", with Ebenezer Scrooge counting his coins while his clerks were shivering, huddled and hungry. If you are able to capture this scene in your head, you would not be off by much if any! Technically speaking the options of translating this phrase while capturing its full meaning is not difficult nor complex.

... deacons must not be *greedy for gain*. Some form of dishonesty is included in the meaning of the term; so NI[87]V "pursuing dishonest gain." It is very likely that deacons were involved in the administration of food and funds to widows and other needy members of the community and therefore were prey to temptations of embezzlement and other forms of dishonesty. In many languages, translators will find TE[88]V's "not greedy for money" a good model. One may also express this as "must not be overly concerned with getting money," or figuratively, "must not be money-hungry."[89]

Many Scriptures are available to us expressing this in both positive and negative terms. For instance:

Now you Pharisees make the outside of the cup and dish clean, but your inward part is full of greed and wickedness.[90]

Therefore I thought it necessary to exhort the brethren to go to you ahead of time, and prepare your generous gift beforehand, which *you had* previously promised, that it may be ready as *a matter of* generosity and not as a grudging obligation.[91]

For I desire mercy and not sacrifice, And the knowledge of God more than burnt offerings.[92]

"Thus says the Lord of hosts: 'Execute true justice, Show mercy and compassion; Everyone to his brother.

---

87 NIV New International Version.

88 TEV Today's English Version

89 Daniel C. Arichea and Howard Hatton, *A Handbook on Paul's Letters to Timothy and to Titus*, UBS Handbook Series (New York: United Bible Societies, 1995), 73.

90 *The New King James Version* (Nashville: Thomas Nelson, 1982), Lk 11:39.

91 *The New King James Version* (Nashville: Thomas Nelson, 1982), 2 Co 9:5.

92 *The New King James Version* (Nashville: Thomas Nelson, 1982), Ho 6:6.

Do not oppress the widow or the fatherless, The alien or the poor. Let none of you plan evil in his heart Against his brother.'[93]

But if you had known what *this* means, '*I desire mercy and not sacrifice,*' you would not have condemned the guiltless.[94]

Most people love to give; certainly, children do. It is a tragic thing when greed grabs the heart of an individual. In many, if not most, Churches the greatest habitual givers are the widow ladies of the Church, and they can least afford to give.[95] Generosity is a great gift to the soul. It improves our disposition and generous people tend to be happier people. When we give, we also need to turn loose our desire to control how the "given money" is used, for once it is given it is no longer ours.

(Another personal experience: are you tired of these?) In a Church where I once served had several wealthy members; they had their own private little club. A couple of deacons were in this informal club as well. About every 5-7 years they would force their unusually successful Pastor to leave. This Church is ideally suited for growth. You could almost dress up a pig and put him in the pulpit and still grow. A new Pastor would come, growth followed and the old crowd said" "Let's let the new people take over some of the responsibilities of leadership". This is the way it should be. Soon the old crowd did not like what was happening. So, the little club would stop giving. They withheld their tithes and offerings. The congregation saw how significantly the income dropped so they voted to scale back the Pastor and staff to part-time. Soon the Pastor had to go elsewhere to support his family. One Pastor made a fight of it, and another Church was started, and it is doing well. And the

---

93   *The New King James Version* (Nashville: Thomas Nelson, 1982), Zec 7:9–10.
94   *The New King James Version* (Nashville: Thomas Nelson, 1982), Mt 12:7.
95   As a pastor I confirm this, and I have never met a Pastor who would dispute this claim.

old Church is now approaching the 5-7 window again. Please pray that God's people will put a stop to this.

For some people, letting go of their tithe is difficult. It is not really a tithe or a gift to the Church if you do not give it completely. It is clear we are to be cheerful givers.

Being wealthy neither qualifies a man to be a deacon nor does poverty disqualify someone from this office. Although, it would be wise to consider the occupation of a deacon candidate. An iffy used car salesman might not be a good choice. A salesman who would "**do anything**" for a sale might not be the best choice for a deacon. Most likely, one who gambles, or a habitual lottery player might not be the best choice as a deacon. Perhaps the most important reason greed is a disqualifier is that deacons may be handling Church money in the performance of their duties. And all Church leaders should ensure they are above reproach when handling Church funds. Reputation plays an important role in this regard.

Here goes the author telling another story.

In a little Church in middle Alabama there were Seven deacons. One of these was Brother Hallman, the finest deacon I have ever met. I was not on staff at this Church, just a member, with my young family. At the time I was attending Samford University using the G.I. bill. On one Sunday, at the close of the service, Brother Hallman asked to speak to the Church. As best as I can remember this is what was said: Brother Hallman was given leave to speak by Brother Ralph Hagood (great preacher, friend, and mentor). Brother Hallman rose from his seat and moved forward to speak and said: "I can no longer serve as your deacon". Many including myself were stunned. I think someone in the congregation asked why? Others moaned and Brother Hallman continued: I have made some poor financial decisions and I am facing bankruptcy. So, lest I bring disrepute upon the Church or the office I hold, I must resign from my position as your deacon. Because of the financial situation I am in I am no longer qualified to be a deacon". Following his resignation many begged him to remain a deacon or to move to inactive status while his finances were settled. But he insisted that he must resign.

You might ask, how is this a GOOD story? Fair question. It showed that Brother Hallman was a **serious-minded deacon** and that he held the Church and congregation in such high esteem that he could not bear to be responsible for bringing shame or embarrassment upon his Church. **He loved his Church so much that he was willing to face public ridicule rather than seeing his Church's witness harmed.** It did not matter to him that no one knew and most likely would never have known the shape of his finances, but he knew. He felt that it was the only **ETHICAL** thing to do. In my years of ministry this is the only instance I have experienced where an active deacon resigned willingly from his service and in public. Brother Hallman will always be remembered as the greatest deacon this author has have ever known.

If I could have written an epithet on Brother Hallman's gravestone I would have written: **DEACON HERO**! The author.

Greed is incompatible with being a good deacon. It opens itself up to the possibility of embezzlement, theft, and other financial crimes. Greed does not always have to do with money. It can manifest itself by wanting to be in the forefront, status, and/or control of people. Manipulative people also are greedy for control, to be in charge and to get their own way. Greed is not just about money. Focusing only on money misses other forms of greed. Perhaps the best way to define this phrase is as: **"not greedy of shameful gain.**[96]**"**

SUMMERY FOR VERSE EIGHT: Deacons need to be Spiritually right, Socially respected, exercise personal discipline, and Financially

---

[96] William Hendriksen and Simon J. Kistemaker, _Exposition of the Pastoral Epistles_, vol. 4, New Testament Commentary (Grand Rapids: Baker Book House, 1953–2001), 130.

right. This does not mean that they are in the upper social class, financially well off. It means in all these areas a deacon must be self-disciplined to be able to restrain his liberties. Consider this:

> A person who does not have this favorable testimony and who is nevertheless chosen to be an overseer in the church may easily "fall into reproach". But here for once "the reproach of the world" is not to the church-member's credit. It is not now an honor, as it is in the other passages where the same word "reproach" is used (Rom. 15:3; Heb. 10:33; 11:26; 13:13). We can imagine how, on the morning after this undeserving person's election to office, the men who work with him will greet him with the mocking exclamation, "What do we hear now? Have they actually made *you* an elder ... *you?*" And *the devil* will rejoice.[97]

It is in the best interest of the Church, of God's Church, the current deacons, the Pastor and ultimately the Kingdom of God that all people of the ministry team are selected and thoroughly meet all the qualifications laid on in Paul's letter to Timothy. There is no substitute for standing on the principles of Scripture.

Verse 9: Most people in the local Church have never considered, in detail, the qualifications for deacons. Likely most Pastors and deacons have not done so either. For many Churches, the only time you hear about deacons is during a deacon election and then during the

---

[97] William Hendriksen and Simon J. Kistemaker, *Exposition of the Pastoral Epistles*, vol. 4, New Testament Commentary (Grand Rapids: Baker Book House, 1953–2001), 129. This is true whether or not the word "reproach" as well as "snare" be construed as modified by "of the devil." Either is grammatically possible, arguments to the contrary (as in Lenski, *op. cit.,* p. 591) notwithstanding. The non-repetition of the preposition (εἰς) argues in favor of linking "of the devil" with both nouns but does not absolutely settle the question. Materially, however, there is little if any difference in meaning. When the world reproaches, the devil, too, reproaches. When Lenski says that the devil is the last one to reproach a Christian for his faults, is he not forgetting Zech. 3:1–3?

installation or commissioning of the new deacon. In verse 8 we saw multiple qualifications and now in verse 9 we have only one.

> ^{NKJV} **⁹holding the mystery of the faith with a pure conscience.**

The English Standard version is remarkably similar to the New King James Version.

> **⁹They must hold the mystery of the faith with a clear conscience.**[98]

The Revised Standard version is closer to the NKJV with very minor word changes.

> **⁹they must hold the mystery of the faith with a clear conscience.**[99]

The New International Version is the most unique translation, but then it also is similar to the previous translations.

> **⁹They must keep hold of the deep truths of the faith with a clear conscience.**[100]

The word "mystery", in our modern world has been linked to many murder mysteries we find on television or in the movies. Often these mysteries require the mind of Sherlock Holmes to unravel them, or perhaps a Mrs. Marple. This is not the case here. Here we are talking about the deep truths of God. We are not talking about the milk of the Word but the meat and potatoes of God's word. The writer of Hebrews lays this out perfectly when he writes:

---

98 *The Holy Bible: English Standard Version* (Wheaton: Standard Bible Society, 2016), 1 Ti 3:9.

99 *The Revised Standard Version* (Oak Harbor, WA: Logos Research Systems, Inc., 1971), 1 Ti 3:9.

100 *The New International Version* (Grand Rapids, MI: Zondervan, 2011), 1 Ti 3:9.

KNJV Hebrews 5:13**For everyone who partakes** *only* **of milk** *is* **unskilled in the word of righteousness, for he is a babe.** **14But solid food belongs to those who are of full age,** *that is,* **those who by reason of use have their senses exercised to discern both good and evil.**

We are talking about men who are solid men of God's Word. They are literate in the Word of God. It has been said that the Word of God is shallow for a child that he may learn in it and so deep that even an elephant can swim in it.[101] These men swim and dive deep, they do not wade. They know how to delve deep into God's word and mine the golden nuggets that God has for HIS people. God has great promises for HIS people, and HE desires they search out HIS Word and draw ever closer.

They understand that Mystery is a "**revealed secret**", meaning that in our context it is a **divine secret** openly revealed to the people of God whereby we call men and women, boys, and girls to Christ Jesus! Men like these stand out especially in Sunday School either as students or teachers. **This should not be surprising, for they know the mysteries of God are the deep truths of God.**

Humility is also a trait that is easily recognizable. God does not leave it to mere chance that the local Church selects the right people to serve HIS Church. God provides ways to recognize the men and their wives HE has set aside for HIS work. The following story is an old one, though it still illustrates the importance and need for Churches to select the right man for the job of deacon.

> When Dr. John Watson was a child, he loved to see the procession of deacons at the administration of the Lord's Supper, and one old man with very white hair and a meek, reverent face especially interested him. One day he was walking on the road and passed a man breaking stones. The white hair caught his

---

101   I am not sure where this is from, but I heard in first while I attended Samford University in Dr. Signard Bryant's classroom.

attention, and he looked back and recognized the deacon who had carried the cup.

Full of curiosity and surprise, he told his father the strange tale. His father explained to him that the reason why the old man held so high a place in the church was that although he was one of the poorest men in all the town, he was one of the holiest. "James," he said, "breaks stones for a living, but he knows more about God than any person I have ever met."[102]

In this real-life story John was captivated by the deacon with "**white hair and a meek, reverent face**". It would be wonderful if all deacons were known in this way. Of course, this story is not Scripture. Nevertheless, we can learn something about deacon ministry from this story. When a believer is touched by the example of a minister, it has a long-lasting effect, either for good or ill. It seems that the media goes out of its way to highlight some sin of some Church leader. But it is almost impossible to find stories of Godly men and women who stand up as a shining example of holiness.

Great deacons make a lifelong impression! In the 1960's there was a Deacon Holcomb (Lakewood Baptist Church, Birmingham, Alabama) who taught a Church Training Class and a Sunday School class for elementary students (the author was in his class); out of that class came one Minister of Music and two Pastors and one Army Chaplain. Great deacons make a great impact for the Kingdom of God. Brother Holcomb taught the Bible and how to use the Bible for daily life. We should all thank God for the people HE brings into our lives to teach and instruct us. Praise God, for He uses us to touch people for HIS Kingdom. In that class, Brother Holcomb taught his boys how to open the Bible and discover God's truths for young lives. He explained the reason the Bible is divided as it is and why it is laid out in such an orderly fashion and most importantly that everything worth knowing is found within its pages.

---

[102] Paul Lee Tan, *Encyclopedia of 7700 Illustrations: Signs of the Times* (Garland, TX: Bible Communications, Inc., 1996), 1630.

SUMMARY OF VERSE NINE: Verse 8 dealt with negative characteristics; in verse 9 Paul turns to the positive: deacons must "keep hold of the deep truths of the faith with a clear conscience." The false teachers have turned away from a good conscience and "have suffered a shipwreck of faith" (1 Timothy 1:5–6, 19–20).[103] This was a problem for Timothy, the young Pastor. At best Timothy faced a situation that shallow Christians, for whatever reason, entered into the servant ministry of the Church and at worst they were satanic infiltrators. It is far better to weed out poor prospects than to remove **BAD** deacons later. Many Churches ordain deacons for **LIFE**! No problem if the deacon ordained turns out to be a great deacon. But if a rotten apple got in, how do you remove the rottenness? The Church must dump out all the apples and look for and remove the rotten apple. This is not a simple thing. This disturbs the Church and embarrasses people needlessly when the Church could have resolved the issue during the selection process. A man of God stands out. It is better to wait for the right man than to choose whoever is left. The importance of following the Biblical process cannot be overly stated.

> Simply because a church member is popular, successful in business, or generous in his giving does not mean he is qualified to serve as a deacon.[104]

It is critical to maintain the Biblical integrity of the Church's deacons by adhering to the Word of God, and in the case of deacons to 1 Timothy 3: 8-12. Unfortunately, this is often not the case. Consider the following:

> I (not the author) have noticed that some church officers know their church constitutions better than they know the Word of God. While it is good to have bylaws and regulations that help maintain order, it is important to manage the affairs of a church based on the Word of God. The Scriptures were the

---

[103] C. Michael Moss, *1, 2 Timothy & Titus*, The College Press NIV Commentary (Joplin, MO: College Press, 1994), 1 Ti 3:9.

[104] Warren W. Wiersbe, *The Bible Exposition Commentary*, vol. 2 (Wheaton, IL: Victor Books, 1996), 222.

"constitution" of the early church! A deacon who does not know the Bible is an obstacle for spiritual growth in a local assembly.[105]

Wow! Imagine what would happen if the Bible were superseded by the bylaws or the constitution of the local Church! What Bible believing Christian would remain? We should flee Churches like that! We need the Holy Spirit, and we need men as servants of the Church.

A little "d" deacon should have a strong understanding of Scripture and put his Biblical knowledge to practical uses. He should be known "as a person of the Bible", he should be able to use the Bible to proclaim the Gospel and he should be inspired to put actions to his beliefs. If a prospective deacon talks about not being called to witness, he should immediately be eliminated from consideration.

What would our Church look like if it had seven deacons who were also lay scholars of the Bible? Would the Church explode in GR0WTH? Would the depth of holiness be amazing?

VERSE TEN is the most practical for the Church. Test, rigorously, prospective deacons.

> **[10]But let these also <u>first be tested</u>; <u>then let them serve as deacons</u>, <u>being *found* blameless</u>.**

This is an example of the common sense found in the Bible. For God trains and provides for HIS servants. This is the way of God. When the qualifications found in 1 Timothy 3 are seriously followed the deacon candidates will be prepared for the work of God. God does not send ill-prepared servants!

> It always weakens the testimony of a local church when a member who has not been proved is made an officer of the church. "Maybe Jim will attend church more if we make him

---

[105] Warren W. Wiersbe, *The Bible Exposition Commentary*, vol. 2 (Wheaton, IL: Victor Books, 1996), 221.

a deacon", is a statement that shows ignorance both of Jim and of the Word of God. *An untested Christian is an unprepared Christian.* He will probably do more harm than good if you give him an office in the church.[106]

The office of deacon should never be given, but earned through testing, displaying a holy and a godly life with a testimony of Christ Jesus. Testing is not showing up and warming a pew or a cushioned seat. Testing is observation over a long period of time examining every aspect of a man's life, including: his homelife, his financial life, his work life and social life. Is he proficient in the Word of God? Is he known as a man of God worthy to be trusted in matters great and small? Does he demonstrate that he knows what a commitment to God means? Is he filled with integrity? Is he just a Church Member or is he involved in ministry regardless of a title?

The idea behind testing is not completely explained. So, we are left to draw from other Scripture tracing how the same words are used in other Pauline passages. And we must trust our translators.

> The nature of the testing is less than clear. Some understand it to be a <u>period of probation</u> (for example, Weymouth "must undergo probation"), or at any rate a <u>formal testing</u> of some kind; TEV[107] can in fact be understood in this way. Others understand it to refer to the practice of designating people who demonstrate the appropriate qualities; these people are **constantly observed**, and it is from them that deacons are selected when necessary. The testing has for its purpose to ***prove themselves blameless***. The term for *blameless* **means "irreproachable"** and is a synonym for **"above reproach"** in 3:2.[108]

---

106 Warren W. Wiersbe, *The Bible Exposition Commentary*, vol. 2 (Wheaton, IL: Victor Books, 1996), 222.

107 TEV Today's English Version

108 Daniel C. Arichea and Howard Hatton, *A Handbook on Paul's Letters to Timothy and to Titus*, UBS Handbook Series (New York: United Bible Societies, 1995), 74.

When taken together we can understand that the period of testing begins when a deacon candidate accepts Jesus Christ as his Savior. In Christian service both character and integrity matter. These men, little "d" deacons, will represent the face of the local Church. Churches need to be careful who represents them!

> **Now to carry out so worthy a task, they, as well as the elders, must be men full of faith and of the Holy Spirit (Acts 6:5).**[109]

Deacons, men of God, must guard their reputations and must be men who are willing to stand and protect the sanctity of deacon service. And focus on ministry and those who can minister. Enlisting men who seem willing and able to meet the qualifications of 1 Timothy to join with them in service will go a long way in demonstrating who is worthy to enter into a profitable deacon ministry.

SUMMARY OF VERSE TEN: Look again at verse 10:

> **But let these also first be tested; then let them serve as deacons, being *found* blameless**

Let us change the phrases around a bit, consider, the following:

> **Let them be tested; being found blameless; then let them serve as deacons.**

To our modern ears this sounds more logical. A variety of Bible translators and Commentary scholars come to the same conclusion though they may use different wording.

> Deacons must **be men of proven worth**. They must "**be tested**". "Unknown" men are not to be appointed to fulfill this task. The testing, a word used for the **testing of a metal** to determine its purity, should make it clear that "there is nothing against" these

---

[109] W Hendriksen and Simon J. Kistemaker, *Exposition of the Pastoral Epistles*, vol. 4, New Testament Commentary (Grand Rapids: Baker Book House, 1953–2001), 130.

men.[110] **Failure to follow this qualification speaks volumes about the local Church that appoints an untested person to the office of deacon**.

A period of testing is done, though methods and the severity of testing varies according to the local Church or the specific denomination. Testing can be very lax or severe. For instance:

The Church of England scrupulously fulfills these directions by requiring "written testimonials, by personal inquiries made by the bishop, by the *Si quis*, by the appeal to the congregation in the Ordination Service, "Brethren, if there be any of you who knoweth any impediment, or notable crime, in any of these persons presented to be ordained deacons, for the which they ought not to be admitted to that office, let him come forth in the name of God, and show what the crime or impediment is;" all well as by the careful examination of the candidates."[111]

These requirements of the Church of England date to 1909 and it is unclear if these unusually strong requirements are still current. One thing is clear: at one time the Church of England took deacon requirements very seriously. It would be wonderful if every Church and every denomination would take a new look at how they choose and test deacons. The expectation is that most Churches seldom insist on such strong requirements. Let us endeavor to follow and adhere to all Scripture, including testing deacon candidates.

> Not only has the example of the foot-washing Lord been treated as a parody, but also, in some instances, the office of deacon has become a seat of power and even abuse. In some traditions it is even pursued as a political office. How far this is from the spirit of Christ! How far from the heart of his followers, and how far from the profile of servants/deacons in 1 Timothy!

---

[110] C. Michael Moss, *1, 2 Timothy & Titus*, The College Press NIV Commentary (Joplin, MO: College Press, 1994), 1 Ti 3:10.

[111] H. D. M. Spence-Jones, ed., *1 Timothy*, The Pulpit Commentary (London; New York: Funk & Wagnalls Company, 1909), 53.

The following list of credentials has everything to do with the gospel.[112]

Testing of deacon candidates is a critical modern-day necessity to weed out those that are found lacking or needful of additional training. Finally let us let the Scripture speak for itself:

> **1 Timothy 5: 22Do not lay hands on anyone hastily, nor share in other people's sins; keep yourself pure.**[113]

When the Scripture speaks it is always best to listen to the Word of God. This is the essence of this little "d" deacon book.

VERSE ELEVEN: Up to this point, all of the deacon qualifications have been deacon specific. Now the wives of prospective deacons will be examined.

¹¹Likewise,

In verse 8 we examined this word; for a refresher look again at verse 8. At this point, though, "Likewise" links verse 11 with the previous passages, which were linked to the passage giving the qualifications of Elders/Pastors.

Their wives

Well, here we go! This is a controversial verse according to scholars and theologians.

The big debate swirling around this verse is whether these qualifications were intended for the wives of deacons or for

---

[112] R. Kent Hughes and Bryan Chapell, *1 & 2 Timothy and Titus: To Guard the Deposit*, Preaching the Word (Wheaton, IL: Crossway Books, 2000), 84.

[113] *The New King James Version* (Nashville: Thomas Nelson, 1982), 1 Ti 5:22.

women who served in the church in some official capacity. We cannot argue too conclusively for either position.[114]

Many Churches passionately reject allowing women to serve in a role that is similar to the role of deacons. Two important TEXT issues argue against this position.

11	Likewise	,	their	wives
	hōsautōs			gynaikas
	hōsautōs			gynē
	autos ōs			gynē

In the above grid we can see what translators had to work with. Notice that no information is given for the word *"their"*. The word *"their"* was inserted in hopes to provide some clarity. It failed to do so but instead blurred the meaning, causing a controversy that continues. The second issue concerns the word **"Likewise"**. This word is used as a transition from one section to another, as we saw when we moved from elders/pastors to our study on deacons. Both issues arise from the ancient text. Because these are textual issues it lends a great deal of weight for scholars to reconsider how this verse is translated and understood. Southern Baptist Churches rarely accept women as deacons. However, these same Churches utilize women in varied important **servant** roles. While **no one is suggesting** that these Churches "**MUST**" radically change WHO can and cannot serve as a deacon, it is fair to acknowledge that godly women who are servants fill a desperately needed role within the Church. In many Churches women provide meals to families who are in a state of bereavement. Cooking, baking, and serving God's people during an exceedingly difficult time is an important ministerial role and touches the basic needs we all have. This ministry was often extended to those outside of the Church family. One woman was so known for baking a cake for funerals that her children referred to the cake as the

---

[114] Knute Larson, *I & II Thessalonians, I & II Timothy, Titus, Philemon*, vol. 9, Holman NT Commentary (Nashville, TN: Broadman & Holman Publishers, 2000), 188.

"dead man's cake[115]". It was very tasty. Women perform all kinds of services to the people in the Church. Cleaning, nursery work, teaching children are just some of the positions of service women commonly provide.

The purpose of this little book is to call Churches to focus on **being** Biblical in all things. And verse 11 is included in that mandate. All of God's words should be considered when forming policies, bylaws, and Church constitutions. Careful consideration for maintaining a Biblical basis for all things should be one of our **HIGHEST PRIORITIES**. Are there arguments for excluding women from the formal deacon ministry? The simple answer is yes. However, none of these arguments are based in the text found within 1 Timothy 3. Nevertheless, they certainly need to be mentioned and are summarized as follows:

> But despite some good arguments, it is a stretch to read in deaconesses here because deacons are the focus mentioned prior to verse 11 and immediately following. Also, the Greek word that can be translated "wife" or "woman" must be translated "wife" in verse 12 ("the husband of but one wife").
>
> Paul is simply telling Timothy that a deacon must have a wife who has acceptability that matches his own, that his wife's qualifications are part and parcel of his qualifications for the office of deacon.[116] Indeed, she will be expected to help him fulfill his duties. **There is immense common sense here** not only as to the nature of marriage in which two become one, but in the strength that a godly couple will bring to a deacon's ministry. The character qualifications of deacons in verse 8 and of the parallel qualifications for their wives in verse 11 ensure

---

[115] Miss Effie's cakes were always good, even the dead man's cake.

[116] George W. Knight, III, *The Pastoral Epistles* (Grand Rapids, MI: Eerdmans, 1992), p. 172.

that they will not only be mutually respectable but will have the same heart for ministry.[117]

This is the view the author holds. From this perspective we would see that "Likewise" transitioning to the wives of deacons fits the context, meaning that we are still talking about deacons but adding the wives as partners in ministry. It would seem unfathomable to have a godly man as a deacon whose wife is mean as a snake. A couple ministry team makes practical sense too. A husband and wife can go places that a husband alone cannot go and the same holds for a godly woman. Together they make a powerful ministry team and because they are together, they keep themselves above reproach. And verse 12 returns to speaking specifically to deacon qualification. Taken together this seems to be the most logical understanding of this verse.

must be reverent,

This has already been discussed earlier. Suffice it to say here is that this woman needs to be worshipful of God.

not slanderers,

This woman needs to be able to keep a secret. The following explanation is more colorful and points to the reason this is so important.

> It is also easily understood why Paul would emphasize that women who do the rounds of the church in performing loving ministries must not be gossipers. "No scandal-mongers please!"

---

[117] R. Kent Hughes and Bryan Chapell, *1 & 2 Timothy and Titus: To Guard the Deposit*, Preaching the Word (Wheaton, IL: Crossway Books, 2000), 86–87. Walter Lock, *The Pastoral Epistles (I & II Timothy and Titus)* (Edinburgh: T. & T. Clark, 1935), p. 40 assesses "the parallelism between the qualities required for them and for the deacons σεμνάς = σεμνούς μὴ διαβόλους = μὴ διαβόλους νηφαλίους = μὴ οἴνῳ πολλῷ προσέχοντας πιστὰς ἐν πᾶσι = μὴ αἰσχροκερδεῖς ··· συνεδὴσει)."

he says as it were. Those who *slander* imitate the evil one, whose very name is *diabolos*, that is, slanderer.[118]

Notice how close **diabolos** is to our English word **diabolical**.

temperate,

Sober, clear headed without non-medicinal stimulants.

faithful in all things.

Consistently standing for Godly things.

Each of these phrases were discussed in more depth earlier in when we were specifically examining deacon qualifications.

VERSE TWELVE:

[12]**Let deacons be the husbands of one wife,**

Here we have another one of those verses that seem amazingly simple to understand. But in our modern immoral and deeply flawed society this is not so easy. Is this one wife at a time? Is this one living wife? What about if he divorced for Biblical reason: adultery for instance? What if he divorced and remarried prior to becoming a Christian? What if he was a deacon who divorced; then remarried; then repented: can he be re-established as a deacon? Each of these cases have perplexed Churches. What is the answer? To resolve these kinds of issues it is important to be kind, loving and Biblically correct! Divorce is increasingly common within the local Church. Although this is the case, this does not mean the qualifications of deacons should be less than the Biblical standards. The Biblical qualifications are the minimum standards. Let the Church never take away or lessen Biblical standards for the Church. **It is better to do without deacons than to lessen the standard.**

---

[118] W Hendriksen and Simon J. Kistemaker, *Exposition of the Pastoral Epistles,* vol. 4, New Testament Commentary (Grand Rapids: Baker Book House, 1953–2001), 133.

When the apostle Paul wrote this letter to Timothy who was serving in Ephesus (This is one of the Churches found in Revelation known as the "Loveless Church").

> **[4]Nevertheless I have *this* against you, that you have left your first love.** [119]

Lust plagued the Roman Empire. So, it is not surprising that there was a need to focus on good families; after all, all the New Testament Churches were planted in a pagan world. We could say the same about today's newly planted Churches. The pagan world had several issues that were anything but family friendly. Polygamy was common in Paul's day, and bigamy was certainly prevalent.[120] Understanding the world that Timothy was ministering in explains the need for a call to be chaste within married life. God's plan for families was first introduced in Genesis with Adam and Eve: one man for one woman for life. This was the ideal. And this is the ideal for deacons.

Additionally, he must be a one-woman man and focus his heart's desire upon her. "No other woman can have his affections maritally, mentally, or emotionally. His wife ought to occupy his full horizon. He must love her as he loves himself. He rejects as treachery anything that would alter his loving focus."[121] He must LOVE his wife, so his daughters and sons will know how to judge prospective spouses. Many books deal with the right relationship between a man and women. In our day where divorce is almost as common as marriage it is important for this high standard to remain intact as a testimony for good marriages.

ruling *their* children

Good loving fathers who care about their children raising good kids. This is another area where deacons are going to be known by how their

---

[119] *The New King James Version* (Nashville: Thomas Nelson, 1982), Re 2:4.

[120] J. Vernon McGee, *Thru the Bible Commentary: The Epistles (1 and 2 Timothy/ Titus/Philemon)*, electronic ed., vol. 50 (Nashville: Thomas Nelson, 1991), 49.

[121] R. Kent Hughes and Bryan Chapell, *1 & 2 Timothy and Titus: To Guard the Deposit*, Preaching the Word (Wheaton, IL: Crossway Books, 2000), 87.

children act and behave in public. Everyone knows who the deacon's children are. This is never a secret. In modern ears "ruling "sounds a bit harsh. A father should shepherd his children. This makes more sense considering the marriage vows: Husbands, love your wives, just as Christ also loved the church and gave Himself for her,[122]. And then we have Ephesians 6: 4; And you, fathers, do not provoke your children to wrath, but bring them up in the training and admonition of the Lord.[123] Fathers, shepherd your children. Husbands, shepherd your wives.

and their own houses well.

The deacon's family must be financially stable. He must be able to manage his resources and still maintain his giving while feeding and clothing his family. This does not mean that he must be rich or well off. He must not be a henpecked husband. A deacon husband must be the family leader. Leading Biblically, pointing his family toward Jesus and being a shining example to the local community.

SUMMARY OF VERSE 12: Deacons are family men. They are the providers and the shepherds of their families. They understand their responsibilities as fathers and husbands. And they are respected because of how they manage their family.

SUMMARY OF QUALIFIATIONS

The word of God must never be treated as other words are treated. God is not like man, for God deeply holds HIMSELF to HIS promises and HIS commands. **God is serious about HIS word:**

> 2 Peter 3; 9 **The Lord is not slack concerning *His* promise, as some count slackness, but is longsuffering toward us, not willing that any should perish but that all should come to repentance.[124]**

---

122 *The New King James Version* (Nashville: Thomas Nelson, 1982), Eph 5:25.
123 *The New King James Version* (Nashville: Thomas Nelson, 1982), Eph 6:4.
124 *The New King James Version* (Nashville: Thomas Nelson, 1982), 2 Pe 3:9.

Habakkuk 2:3 **For the vision *is* yet for an appointed time; But at the end it will speak, and it will not lie. Though it tarries, wait for it; Because it will surely come, It will not tarry.**[125]

Summarizing the importance of God's Word can be found in Psalms 119; one writer sees the following within this important Psalm.

> *God's **Word is sure** (119:89–96):* 119:89–96. God's ***Word is settled*** in heaven and is attested by His **faithfulness** (vv. 89–91). The psalmist's **delight** (cf. 1:2; 119:174) in the established **Law** had enabled him to win the victory (vv. 92–95). He concluded that God's Word is **boundless** (v. 96) in its values.[126]

God's word is valuable to all people of all ages; this includes Churches and denominations. Read and be changed by God's word. It is folly to try to bend God's Word to modern cultural norms and hope that it will satisfy a Holy God. Keep the focus on obedience to God's Word and combine with a people seeking God's will; surely the Holy Spirit will present the right man.

---

[125] *The New King James Version* (Nashville: Thomas Nelson, 1982), Heb 2:3.

[126] Allen P. Ross, "Psalms," in *The Bible Knowledge Commentary: An Exposition of the Scriptures*, ed. J. F. Walvoord and R. B. Zuck, vol. 1 (Wheaton, IL: Victor Books, 1985), 881.

CHAPTER 7

Practical Issues for
Little "d" deacons

D eacon ministry is an essential ministry for a growing and/or for a persecuted Church. In both instances we can readily see why both situations require little "d"deacons. In the case of the former an ever-expanding ministry in a growing Church requires a need for deacons to multiply the ministry efforts of their Pastor. And in the case of the latter a persecuted Church needs deacons for continuity. In areas that persecute Christians, the Pastors are often the first to face arrest, imprisonment, or assignation. This was the methodology of the Nazi regime during Hitler's holocaust. It is a similar methodology in some states in India and in parts of Africa.

A growing Church

A growing Church needs little "d" deacons, especially Churches which are in a state of transition along the life scale of the Church. Churches develop and grow at different rates: alternately growing, reaching a plateau, declining and growth. Some Churches remain at different stages for different times. Of course, The life cycle of the Church is not fixed science. Some Churches only last a generation and make a powerful impact for God's Kingdom. Fourth Avenue North Baptist Church in Birmingham, Alabama was such a Church. In its short life span it produced writers for the Women's Missionary Union, Missionaries, Pastors and at least one Army Chaplain. The life cycle of a Church is highly subjective but also provides a basic understanding of how Churches grow or not grow, or grow for a while and then plateau, and sometimes die is necessary to evaluate where our Churches are. Some Churches start as a small family Church and never progress much beyond that a family church. Others start as a Missionary effort. Other transition from a family Church to a small Church and on to a medium size Church. This is where so many Churches stop growing and this is where little "d" deacons can make a dramatic impact. This is not to say that little "d" deacons can only make an impact in medium size Churches. Great deacons can make an impact anywhere God plants them. **Great little "d" deacons impact the Church, the community, and Great Commission for God's glory.**

In a small Church or a family Church, deacons are either going to be related to most of the Church members or everyone will be well known by him. This is also true in the local community. Deacons are often cited as a reason why people do not go to the deacon's Church. Small Churches and family Churches are very well equipped to minister to each other for very few secrets can be kept in such a tight group; again, this also applies to the local community. Small and family Churches are loving communities of worshiping believers who know how to minister to one another. Family churches do have a weakness: sometimes failing new members. It is difficult for a new member to be integrated into all levels of the Church community. In Churches such as these two or three deacons are usually more than enough to manage the ministries that the part time Pastor cannot manage. These small and family Churches have trained many of our modern-day Pastors[127] (including this author). It is these Godly people who have sat patiently through many poorly delivered and constructed messages. These wonderful, blessed Church people and deacons representing these Churches of God have helped many young Pastors mature and develop into men of God preaching and proclaiming Jesus to a desperate World. The local Church will never know how many Pastors, Missionaries, Seminary Professors, and a host of other workers for the Kingdom of God who were trained in

---

[127] The author will always be thankful for Mount Zion Baptist Church, just outside of Centerville, Alabama and Fourth Avenue North Baptist Church in Birmingham, AL

small Churches. These Churches have a place in the kingdom of God, sometimes humbly listening to beginner Preachers who will one day have their part to play in worldwide evangelism. Thank God for these small Churches that ministered to God's people all over the world. Almost every large Church has had a Pastor who first started out in a small, humble Church. God uses Churches of every size to fulfill the great commission. Praise God for the many small Churches.

Small Churches are often the underrated heroes of most denominations. Small Churches have played a powerful role in Church history in helping to develop men and women for ministry. These small Churches are unbelievably forgiving and patient people loving a string of ministers and raising up young people who populate many larger Churches. God honors small Churches, for they reach to the most distant Mission fields.

> The small church, writes Anthony G. Pappas, is "a single cell of caring people. It does not exist to do, as the mid-sized-program church does. It exists to be. Its essence is not in its administrative structure, charismatic leadership, and long-range plans, as is the case in the large church."[128]

In the small Church community **love** is the driving force. **Small Churches know how to love** one another and their many Pastors. Little "d" deacons in Churches like these know how to demonstrate love for one another and have an unexpected gift of generosity. In Mount Zion Baptist Church in Centerville, Alabama there were two men who personified little "d"deacons in the early 1980s. Brother James and Brother Roy were humble men of God. They both had keen insight into the needs of the local Church and their community and met many of them out of their own pockets. They knew what ministry should be and they did their duty. These men are heroes of the Church.

---

[128] John Koessler, "Investing in Small-Church Futures," in *Renewing Your Church through Vision and Planning: 30 Strategies to Transform Your Ministry*, ed. Marshall Shelley, vol. 2, Library of Leadership Development (Minneapolis, MN: Bethany House, 1997), 232.

These two men were my (author's) first deacons. They allowed their Pastor to lead the Church and quietly behind the scenes helped their Pastor make wise decisions. These two men never corrected this Preacher boy in public or in front of the Church. I learned more about ministry from these two fine men of God than all three years of Seminary. Even though these men of God are now with Jesus, I still thank God for knowing them.[129]

Godly deacons touch people. They touch pastors and distant Churches where these pastors will later serve. Neither of the two deacons knew that one of their pastors would go on to serve in the US Army as an Army Chaplain.

Godly men have a long reach. Their ministry touches lives, families, and churches that they never hear about. Their guidance and encouragement go a long way when young preacher boys begin. How many churches did these men touch by training Pastors for other Churches? Brother Roy and Brother James have passed away, but their positive touch on other Pastors continues right up to the Throne of God. What diadems have they won for Christ Jesus? These men are heroes of the faithful.

The small Church is the training ground from which God usually recruits men and women of God into expanded ministries. This does not mean that larger Churches do not touch lives and raise up men and women to serve. However, there are far more small churches than large ones. In a small Church boys and girls can see their Pastor and likely he knows their names. Small Churches and their Pastors have more time to spend on individuals and invest in the eternity of their lives. Programs

---

[129] During Brother Jerry McGowin's first pastorate. Brother Roy told me it was time for me to move on to seminary. He told me I had too much to offer the Kingdom of God to remain in a small Church. Then Brother Roy wrote me a Check that was enough money to get my family and myself to New Orleans Baptist Seminary. I thank God for having known Brother Roy and Brother James. For God used these two men to change my life. I personally know two other Pastors that Brother Roy and Brother James helped both of which moved on to larger Southern Baptist Churches. I am eternally grateful to Brother Roy and Mrs Effie who have both gone on to be with the Lord Jesus.

are less important that investing in the lives of people. This is a ministry to the much wider Believers Community. Every Church, regardless of its size, is God's Church. This is not some platitude but the reality of God's Kingdom. Every Church has a part to play in the Kingdom of God. Not every Church meets every need, yet many Churches can meet many needs. It would be a mistake to think or believe that our particular Church is indispensable to God's plan. God does not need us; it is us who need God. It is a good day when we can say it is good to be an obedient servant to a Holy and Just God.

Let us be grateful that God has chosen us to be servants in HIS Kingdom. We must not allow ourselves to think we are in competition with other Churches. We should focus on being obedient to the word of God. This is the essential duty of all believers, including the Pastor and little "d" deacons.

A growing Church is a Church that is growing both numerically and spiritually but, numbers alone are not the true measure of a growing Church. To understand a growing Church, we have no need to look outside of Scripture.

> All . . . qualities found in the early church at Jerusalem had one important consequence—it was a growing church. Christian leaders today are greatly concerned about church growth, and rightly so. Many formulas have been suggested to achieve this growth. Every one of these formulas may have some value, but the church at Jerusalem, without any scientific studies or volumes of statistics, had a successful formula. Their total commitment led to a joyous and winsome lifestyle that proved irresistible to those outside its ranks.[130]

The Jerusalem Church faced many difficulties. Fear of the dominate religion – Jews. Legitimate fear of the local leadership – Pharisees, Sadducees, Jewish Priesthood, and the Sanhedrin. They lived in an

---

[130] John W. Wade, *Acts: Unlocking the Scriptures for You*, Standard Bible Studies (Cincinnati, OH: Standard, 1987), 33.

occupied nation with the growing presence of the Roman Army. Persecution was a daily reality. In this environment the Church continued to grow.

This is the mark of a growing Church! And one element of the explosive growth in the early Jerusalem Church was the beginning of the little "d" deacon ministry. Remember: [Acts 6:6]**whom they set before the apostles; and when they had prayed, they laid hands on them. ⁷Then the word of God spread, and the number of the disciples multiplied greatly in Jerusalem, and a great many of the priests were obedient to the faith.**[131] This testimony from the book of Acts gives us the formula for a growing Church:

1: Total commitment to Jesus Christ
2: An expectation that God is at work in the World.

It seems odd to waste money for research and studies to discover what it takes to grow a Church. Why do we accept the word of "experts" when we are called to be Holy men and women of God? Policies and programs are poor substitutes for a Church wrapped in holiness and prayer. We also have evidence that the Church in Jerusalem was not unique in its explosive growth. For instance:

> The New Testament survives intact because of the thousands of manuscripts copied by scribes for a growing church over the centuries. Historical works from the major ancient historians such as Josephus, Tacitus, and Pliny survive on just a handful of copies, and those copies are hundreds of years from the originals. Why do the skeptics think anything is going to be written, much less survive, from an ancient group of illiterate Galilean peasants?[132]

---

[131] *The New King James Version* (Nashville: Thomas Nelson, 1982), Ac 6:6–7.
[132] Norman L. Geisler and Frank Turek, *I Don't Have Enough Faith to Be an Atheist* (Wheaton, IL: Crossway Books, 2004), 248.

In a world devoid of computers, newspapers, mass media and increasing Christian opposition including persecution **the written Word of God flourished**. The growing early Church, used of God, prepared the way for believers in our present age to hold the Word of God in our hands. This is a mighty gift. And yet it is too often tossed in the back seat of the car until next Sunday or worse still left on the shelf to gather dust. We believers have in our midst a powerful spiritual weapon, though seldom used. Let us become the People of the Book once again. Let us focus on reading the Word of God in our homes, at our schools and in our places of work. Let the Pastor preach the Word of God systematically. Let the little "d" deacons become mighty in the Word of God and inspire a new generation for Revival in God's Churches, all the while showing those outside of the Kingdom what the Kingdom of God represents.

> The mentality of a growing church is continually one of reaching out to others. Even the personal development of current members will be seen in light of increasing their ability to care genuinely about others and minister to them. The minute we start to plan for others rather than ourselves, we create a climate in which we develop, and the church will grow.[133]

Well said! Jesus extolled the role of servant. And it is deacons who can most readily project this mentality of servanthood. A Church that focuses on serving one another speaks volumes to the local community. This concept was proven by the early Jerusalem Church. Being a servant runs counter to our society that values celebrities, fame, status, and wealth. A culture that lives to be served rather than serve. The religious leadership and the Pharisees we see portrayed in Scripture do not seem too different when compared to our modern culture. Both want/wanted to be honored by men rather than by God. This is a failure of the world but must not be a failure within the Church. A local Church that is blessed with little **"d"** servant deacons is indeed a blessed Church and can focus on the Word of God and reaching the desperate.

---

[133] Larry K. Weeden, ed., _The Magnetic Fellowship: Reaching and Keeping People_, vol. 15, The Leadership Library (Carol Stream, IL; Waco, TX: Christianity Today, Inc.; Word Books, 1988), 37.

Jesus clearly pictured for us that we are to serve one another. Truly it is better to serve than be served. Jesus, speaking of Himself, said: NKJV Mark 10: 45**For even the Son of Man did not come to be served, but to serve, and to give His life as a ransom for many.** Jesus, by example, showed us that serving others is the **Master's** way. This should not be confusing to us. And yet few Churches are making a genuine effort to serve God's people and to serve those outside the Community of Faith. Why is this the case in many Churches? It is unlikely that this question can ever be answered! Nevertheless, we must move from thinking about the question of why and move to the question of HOW! The first step is to encourage one another in a life of service, both great and small. Spending more money is not the answer. **In fact, money is never the issue**. More programs are not the answer. The clear answer is to re-acquaint us to the Bible and to a prayerful life. Or to state this is in another way: we need revival to begin first with our individual Church's leadership. Let the little "d " deacons come before the Church and say: "Let us serve God's people." A defining character of a Church in God's will is love and service. One without the other is a lie.

Jesus spoke to the poor people and ministered almost exclusively to God's Chosen people (Jews) and almost all of these were poor. One, possibly a widow, had spent all she had on medical treatments and came to Jesus as a desperate last attempt to be healed. Others had broken bodies or limbs that no longer worked or eyes that could no longer see. Jesus was a healer and a walking Hospital and the last desperate hope of many. Jesus served HIS people. And clearly, we are to be more like Jesus. The following illustration presents a correct Biblical understanding of service. When we serve the Church or the poor, are we really serving Jesus? We are! Because we are being obedient to his example and HIS word!

> --A poor man lived near Deacon Murray, referred to in the tract, "Worth a Dollar, " and occasionally called at his house for a supply of milk. One morning he came when the family were at breakfast. --Mrs. Murray rose to wait upon him, but the deacon said to her, "wait till after breakfast. "She did so, and meantime

the deacon made some inquiries of the man about his family and circumstances. After family worship the deacon invited him to go out to the barn with him. When they got into the yard, the deacon, pointing to one of the cows, exclaimed, "There, take that cow and drive her home." The man thanked him heartily for the cow, and started for home, but the deacon was observed to stand in the attitude of deep thought until the man had gone some rods.--He then looked up and called out, "Hey, bring that cow back." The man looked around, and the deacon added, "Let that cow come back, and you come back, too." He did so, and when he came back into the yard again the deacon said, "There, now take your pick out of the cows. I ain't going to lend to the Lord the poorest cow I've got!"[134]

We can see how Deacon Murry's thinking changed: 1. His first thought was to provide some milk; 2 Then to give away the poorest cow he had and 3. Finally to give away the pick of the litter. The poor man came hoping for some milk and left blessed with a cow. This is not too different from how we come to Jesus. We come to Jesus hoping and praying and believing Jesus will give us PEACE and instead of just receiving PEACE we are abundantly blessed with unspeakable JOY too. When we first asked Jesus into our hearts, we had no idea what that would really mean. Jesus meets us where we came to HIM and Jesus moved us to an even better place and promised us an inheritance in Heaven. Which Jesus has purchased and prepared for us. Jesus did not stop serving us when we were saved. HE continues to work for us throughout our lives. Working even now in the life of every believer. Jesus has never stopped serving HIS people. Is it not fair to say, the moment we are saved Jesus begins an eternal commitment to serve us? Jesus loves HIS people, and HE has promised to return for us.

Summary of Practical Issues of a growing Church. A growing Church is moving in the right direction and should be commended. Growth should be monitored. Are the people growing Spiritually? Are deacons

---

[134] Richmond Dispatch, _The Daily Dispatch: 1865_, Richmond Daily Dispatch (Richmond, Virginia: Perseus Digital Library, 1865).

serving the church in ministry? The public face of the Church is often deacons. Does the local community see the Church's deacon in a good light? If not, they will not see the local Church in a good light either. Be sure we are not confusing administrative functions as ministry. Anyone can open a door. Serving in a committee is administrative work, not ministry. Church membership makes some demands on the congregation too. In many Churches a brick or a rock can hold open a door. But it takes a person to minister! Are you a ROCK or a minister within the Church? We have all been called to be servants.

A persecuted Church, though it may be growing, has significantly different needs than a growing Church where persecution is extremely limited or unknown. In the case of the persecuted Church, Pastors are often the first target. This was the case in Nazi Germany prior to entry of the United States into World War II. Internment Camps, Death Camps, Detention Camps were not limited to Jews. Many evangelicals, along with many others also suffered under the hands of the ruthless "SS" agents of Hitler. These Nazis cared very little for their charges. "During the Nazi regime in Germany before the war and during the Nazi occupation of such countries as Holland after 1939, it became obvious that a church whose ministry was confined to what the clergy could do was hopelessly inadequate to the demands of the times."[135] The bravest and most influential Pastors who stood and boldly resisted the Nazi movement were conscripted into the Army or were arrested and confined for the duration of the war. Dietrich Bonhoeffer was one of these. In Dietrich's case Hitler ordered Dietrich's execution as one of his final acts as Chancellor of Germany. Men like Pastor Bonhoeffer soon disappeared from the German Public Square. And the institutional Church was left without bold leadership!

> The Nazis did not object to people gathering for worship, let alone to an individual worshiping on his own. Preaching could be continued in such a way as to be **unobjectionable**. What

---

[135] Francis O. Ayres, The Ministry of the Laity: A Biblical Exposition, page 11. The United Methodist Church 1200 Davis Street, Evanston, Illinois 60201. Library of Congress Catalog Card Number 62-10295

the Nazis could not and would not tolerate was worship and preaching that resulted in action contrary to their (Nazi) wishes.[136]

History is repeating itself again. It seems to that people are forgetting our history. More and more so-called preachers of the Gospel are preaching **UNOBJECTIONABLE**[137] messages to the Churches.

Those who cannot remember the past are condemned to repeat it.[138]

Recently a Christian florist, Barronelle Stutzman, and a Christian Baker, Jack Phillips, were targeted by anti-Christian leftist groups for their refusal to be willing participants in morally objectionable practices. In both cases lower courts ruled against them. The basic argument against them was they did not have the freedom, based on their Christian Faith, to deny them from choosing not to associate with celebrations of homosexual unions. In other words, if their faith were private and not **publicly objectionable,** they were free to worship; but their Christianity could not influence their business decisions. In both cases their livelihoods were threatened with severe civil penalties if they continued to stand for Jesus Christ. Christ Jesus is our Lord and Savior and as Lord He claims our life (all of it) for Himself. Therefore, it is reasonable to understand that Jesus expects that our Christian expression is seen in all forms of our life, including: Homelife, Work life, Social life, School life as well as our Faith life.

Pastors and little "d" deacons need to minister as if persecution is imminent. There are places in our world where the Pastor's replacement is called as soon as a Church installs its new Pastor. In places like these the Pastor's life expectancy may be as little as two years or three years. In situations like these deacons are crucial. When the heavily persecuted Church is forced underground, it will be deacons who will be expected

---

[136] Ibid, page 14.
[137] **UNOBJECTIONABLE,** if Christians are unobjectionable, they are like salt that has lost it flavor. This is what our culture is trying to do to believers, beat us down until we are **UNOBJECTIONABLE!**
[138] George Santayana, American Philosopher.

to take up the slack in ministry. This is why it is so crucial that Churches elect and install little "d" deacons. Francis O. Ayres examined what happens to Churches whose Pastors were stripped away from their congregations and his conclusion was that:

> The world needs Christian lay people in the power centers more than the Church needs badge wearers.[139]

Mr. Ayres context was not specifically talking about deacons but the general membership of the Church. But his point is easily understandable. A title or status in the Church is not nearly as effective as having Christians involved in government, military, business, politics, and education. The Church clearly needs revival that extends outside of the Church building, infecting our culture for the cause of Jesus Christ. All of us are called to change the world for Jesus and to accomplish this task we need some radical thinking regarding what the Church is involved in. The Church requires a radical reordering. A return to Biblical thinking and preaching. We need to escape constantly restricting our expectations that the latest program will turn around the fortunes of our Churches. Programs and/or a younger Pastor is a poor substitute for evangelism. Jesus provided a clear mandate for the Church:

NKJV Mark 16: 15 And He said to them, "Go into all the world and preach the gospel to every creature.

When the Church or the Church's leadership departs from this mandate then we are out of touch with Jesus and His view of the Church. Keeping the doors open in a dying Church IS NOT evangelism but pointing people to Jesus is. Every believing Church member is a minister of Jesus Christ, weather they are good or bad. All believers reflect on Jesus. And all of God's ministers are called to proclaim Jesus, not just in the Church but on the roadside and at work. Some families ban the discussion of Politics and Religion at family events. This seems to be a growing trend. If we cannot talk to our family about Jesus, who can

---

[139] Francis O. Ayres. Page 19.

we talk to? The sad truth is we seldom talk to anybody about Jesus. Is it any wonder our world has gone mad?

Now, if everyone is a minister in the Church family and out of that little "d" deacons are called to be servants how much more powerful are the stories about Stephen and Philip who were two of the first seven deacon. Let us have a little review.

NKJV Acts 6: 7 **Then the word of God spread, and the number of the disciples multiplied greatly in Jerusalem, and a great many of the priests were obedient to the faith.**

This verse followed the calling of the first seven deacons. Deacon ministry was so positive and impactful that it spurred many Jewish priests to accept Jesus Christ as Lord. This **CANNOT BE** a coincidence. Biblical deacon ministry ignited an evangelism effort that took Jerusalem by storm. Notice the wording of this verse. It was not some priests or many priests, but a **GREAT MANY PRIESTS** came to a believing faith in Jesus. How did this happen? It happened because the Church was so excited about this ministry that they began to talk about it to friends and neighbors. Widows and orphans who had been begging at the temple no longer were there and when the Jewish priests learned what was happening, they were moved by the Holy Spirit and saw that the people of the Church were doing a great work for God. But how is this tied to the Mandate of Jesus that we should go unto all the world and preach the Gospel?

> Paul Lowenberg preached, "The mandate of the church is generally considered in the words of Jesus, 'Go into all the world, and preach the gospel to every creature.'
>
> - Webster says a mandate is 'a formal order from a superior court to an inferior one: an authoritative command, an injunction or order.'

- Our mandate is not a matter of interpretation; it is a matter of total obedience to the last will and testament of the Lord Jesus Christ[140]

This is not one of those verses that the interpretation makes a difference! The mandate of Christ is crystal clear. There is no need to see through a glass darkly here. Two of the first seven deacons knew the importance of this mandate: Stephen died for it and Philip was moved by God to chase Chariots. Any deacon worth his salt knows these stories.

Interestingly, Stephen had no converts, but Philip did. The other five deacons we know nothing about. This seems to suggest that Stephen and Philip should be the models for deacon ministry. If someone believes differently it would be interesting to hear their Biblical based argument that Stephen and Philip should not be the model!

Philip and Stephen were both deacons in a growing Church with problems. They were also deacons in a persecuted Church and still they **PUBLICLY** preached the Gospel of Jesus. This is where the World is trending: Worldwide persecution is coming and has already begun. If there is any doubt about a coming Worldwide persecution of the Church, then examine https://www.persecution.com/ or better yet attend one of the Voice of the Martyrs Conferences. _Tortured for Christ — The Complete Story;_ is another great story of the persecuted, how one Pastor was tortured for Christ for 17 years. These are not just stories. These are stories of believers who face imprisonment, torture, and death daily for the cause of Jesus. It would be a mistake to think it will not happen here. If the persecuted Church mattered to our Nation or to the United Nations, then a collective effort would be launched to stop the persecution of the Church. Is this kind of persecution coming here? It is coming, it is here --there can be no doubt!

Persecution is coming to us. It could happen under the next president or under the next Congress. The moral divide in the US is growing.

---

[140] 60 Seconds - The Mandate of the Church; Global Christian Center; http://globalchristiancenter.com.

How long has the Church lamented about the removal of God from Public Education. The Church did nothing about it. The Church had better WAKE UP and vote to protect Religious Liberty in our Country. Persecution could be only one vote away. It does not take a prophetic eye to see persecution is coming. All one needs to do is look at the news one evening and see how the Nation is moving away from God at an alarming rate. If we need more evidence, then read the seven letters in Revelation. Is it possible to see the present in the past? Fear can move the government to act in a radical way. Internment camps, segregation, creating second class citizens: Our Government has done this before. This was done following the Civil War and following the attack on Pearl Harbor leading to our national involvement in World War II. One crisis could hurl the American Church into a full-blown era of persecution.

Summary of the practical issues of the persecuted Church. Little "d" deacons in a persecuted Church are crucial. Persecuted Churches are under constant threat that their Pastor will disappear or suffer intense persecution. The Church could become shepherd-less in the middle of the night or suddenly while he is walking down the street. What then? Little "d" deacons will be left to minister alone; likely they will have to move underground to continue the ministry of the Church. This is what is happening in places we regularly see in the nightly news. China is arresting and closing Churches and destroying Church buildings at an alarming rate. Indonesia is actively persecuting Christians. In some states in the nation of India the police turn a blind eye when Christians are persecuted by the local populace. Brave Pastors who are fulfilling the Great Commission of Jesus do not survive long when they boldly preach the living Jesus. In Churches like these it is deacons who hold the Christian community together. Following the persecution of the Pastor, then soon persecution will extend to little "d" deacons.

Pray for deacons who live under the constant threat of persecution. Pray for the persecuted Church.

A stagnant Church needs a revival fire. It needs a radical change in direction. It needs a purifying fire from God.

> NKJV Revelation 3: 15 **"I know your works, that you are neither cold nor hot. I could wish you were cold or hot. ¹⁶So then, because you are lukewarm, and neither cold nor hot, I will vomit you out of My mouth.**

These words of Jesus should be terrifying words to a stagnant Church. All Churches should examine where they are before the Lord. The Lord's Supper calls us to examine our individual selves. Why not take two or three weeks prior to the next Lord's Supper to call the Church to examine itself. Re-evaluate programs, policies, Church Constitution and the Bylaws of the Church. Are they in line with Scripture and the example of Jesus? Should we re-align our Sunday School classes to better allocate our Church's resources? Are we ministering to the poor directly or are we just giving money for others to do the job? Are we personally involved in serving others? These are just a few questions to begin a thorough examination of our Church.

> Veikko Manninen of Finland said, "Some ask, 'How will God handle the one who has never heard the Gospel?' The more important question (for the Church) is, **'How will God handle the one who has disobeyed God's command to go into all the world and preach the Gospel?"**[141]

The stagnant Church must do something, anything. Selling the property and giving it to Missions is better than sitting in a do-nothing Church building. The stagnant Church can do one of two things: dry up and die or do something for Jesus. There are no other options, consider this:

> Oswald J. Smith warned, "Any church that is not seriously involved in helping to fulfill the Great Commission has forfeited its biblical right to exist." A famous artist was once

---

[141] Veikko Manninen, contributor to: **The New International Dictionary of Pentecostal and Charismatic Movements.**

asked to paint a picture of a dying church. It was expected that he would paint a small and humble building. Instead, he painted a stately edifice with a rich pulpit and magnificent windows--and near the door, an offering box marked MISSIONS, with the contribution slot blocked by a cobweb![142]

The stagnant Church is inward looking. The stagnant Church asks: Why does no one come? Or they ask: Why are they here? The stagnant Church only cares about its own. They come for fellowship; they come to their own private club. They have ceased to be a Biblical Church. Too many of these Churches exist. The book of Revelation calls these Churches Laodicean Churches – neither hot nor cold.

In marriage counseling, the counsellor will often try and determine where the couple is at in their relationship. They will often try to measure the opposition of one to the other. Couples that love one another can be helped to make their marriages better. Even couples that have hate for one another can often be helped. They can be helped because they still have enough personal investment in the relationship to still be able to have strong emotional connections with one another. Hate is not the opposite of Love. However, if couples are indifferent to one another then emotional attachments have all been severed. They may continue to live together, but no longer as a husband and wife. At best, they are occupying a space together. This was the case of the Laodicean Church: it was indifferent to the cause of Jesus Christ.

Summary of a stagnant Church. They are no longer a Biblical Church; they are a Church and a people awaiting judgment.

The Churches' constitution and bylaws. Church constitutions and bylaws are primarily restrictive documents. Often, they may hinder deacons from ministering. Some Churches' Constitutions and bylaws require deacons to serve on certain committees, or worse yet, require deacons to be the committee chairmen. Serving on a committee is

---

[142] Dave Arnold, Pastor: Gulf Coast Worship Center, New Port Richey, Florida. www.davidarnoldonline.org

an administrative role and this is not the Biblical role for a deacon. A deacon may serve on a committee as a Church member but let us not confuse the two roles.

This is an easy fix. But often it seems impossible. To remove deacons as a chairman of a committee or as a committee member separates that deacon from power, influence, and prestige. For this to happen somewhat painlessly deacons need to make this a recommendation to the Church. This will accomplish at least two things: new people will become Committee members and **the new message to the Church is deacons are servants** not administrators. A very important distinction.

Naturally, a simple vote from the Church can change the constitution and/or bylaws. If this is done the congregation will need an explanation as to why this change is recommended. One way to do this is to present to the congregation **what the deacons' new focus will be.** Opposition is likely to come from Big "D" deacons as they will likely oppose this change in the deacon meeting. If this hurdle can be overcome, then the process is likely to happen smoothly and with little notice or fanfare. Most congregations can readily read Acts 6 and 1 Timothy 3 for guidance and Scripture usually prevails in Evangelistic Churches.

A change of this magnitude should be planned for and thoroughly discussed by all the deacons and the Pastor. It is preferable to have a united front and if it fails the first time there is always next year. Many Churches allow for deacon recommendations during every business meeting, and this is a good practice, especially if the focus is on ministry. And it is here that a recommendation to remove deacons from their administrative roles required by the Constitution and/or Bylaws can be made. It is suggested that any recommendation should be presented in writing so that it can be immediately inserted into the Bylaws and Constitution. Additionally, deacons, after consulting with the trustees could recommend that the trustees take over the deacons' role in committee meetings. Trustees are a natural fit to serve as either a committee person or as chairman of committees that oversee the budget, payroll, or other financial matters of the Church. Separating deacons from the finances of the Church frees them to focus on ministry.

Summary: constitutions and bylaws. Most Churches have trustees to represent the Church in all legal matters. Moving trustees into a role where they will exercise some supervision over the monies of the Church seems like a natural fit. Often trustees are trusted members of the Church, usually with some business or accounting background. These men and women would be familiar with budgets and the financial requirements necessary to operate under the Law. Of course, the Church would need Godly people to hold this position. And it would give opportunities for men and women who are not normally eligible to serve as deacons an opportunity to serve in the local Church.

Deacon Ministry has an implied role and an explicit role. <u>Ministering to widows is the key ministry role for deacons</u> and the **only one EXPLICITLY presented in Scripture**. This explicit ministry is the **SOLE REASON EXPLICITLY STATED IN SCRIPTURE.** Again, we must return to Acts 6.

> NKJV Acts 6: 2**Then the twelve summoned the multitude of the disciples and said, "It is not desirable that we should leave the word of God and <u>serve tables</u>. 3 Therefore, brethren, seek out from among you seven men of *good* reputation, full of the Holy Spirit and wisdom, whom we may <u>appoint over this business</u>. . .**

Three key elements concerning the ministry of deacons can readily be seen in these two verses. The complaint in the Church was simply this: some of the widows were not being provided for. Once again this was the **ONLY explicit** reason given for the existence of deacon ministry. Secondly, it was the apostles/pastors who appointed deacons to the ministry, NOT the congregation. Thirdly, deacons have a secondary role that is implied in this passage. See Acts 6:2.

NKJV Acts 6:2_Then the twelve summoned the multitude of the disciples and said, "It is not desirable that we should leave the word of God and serve tables._

Deacons have a role to protect the Pastor's time that is set aside for study and preparation for the presentation of Scripture to God's people. This is THE key role for Pastors. Ideally every Pastorate should be full time. But this is usually not financially or geographically possible. If the Pastor is serving in a part time position, then this implied role of deacons is even more important. The Pastor must have time to study and prepare.

Based on Acts 6 deacons have an **EXPLICIT** role and an **IMPLIED** role to play within the Church. The reality of Pastoral ministry is there is never enough time for the Pastor to do all the things necessary for a healthy Church. Visitation to the homebound, the hospital, walking with families through grief, deaths of a loved one both within and without the Church. Community involvement is another time stealer for many Pastors. Pastors must be free to work during the day and the night and weekends, he is constantly on call. He usually has a wife and children who also have needs. Likely he has parents and an extended family where he is usually the first call when his extended family is in crisis. He is the first call to come and do a family funeral regardless of the distance. Deacons are crucially important in protecting the Pastor's time.

The qualifications in First Timothy are important to follow, for deacons need to be self-starters and energetic about ministry. They need to be men who require a minimum of supervision. They need to be men of strong character who can stand firm on Biblical Principles. Deacon ministry is not an easy ministry. But when done well deacons and their Pastor form a bond in ministry that can last a lifetime. Churches with a healthy deacon ministry will often find that the Pastor's best friend in the Church is a deacon. Pastors need friends and a Pastor can have no better friend than one who shares his passion about ministry. Deacons need to take care of their Pastor as one friend would do for another.

Deacons should be protectors of the Pastor's study and prayer time.
  Questions Deacons should ask:
    Does my pastor look or seem tired?
    Does my pastor look or seem troubled?

Deacons should be protectors of the Pastor's family time.
  Questions Deacons should ask:
    Does my pastor's wife seem tired or troubled?
    Are all the physical needs of my Pastor's family being met?
    Deacons should be protectors of the Pastor's Ministry time and
    be protectors of the Pastor's Teaching time.

  Questions Deacons should ask:
    What will we do to lighten our Pastor's burden?
    What will we do to ease our Pastor's burden?
    What will we do as deacons to assist our Pastor?
    What needs will our Pastor have that we can anticipate?

Deacons are involved in ministry. There is no one else in the Church that is more qualified than a little "d" deacon to minister to the Pastor. A little "d" deacon understands the weight of ministry, for they have felt it themselves. This is a sacred trust that deacons have with their Pastor. And when a deacon betrays a Pastor's confidence it seems, to the Pastor, that he realizes to some degree what Jesus felt when Judas betrayed Jesus with a kiss. Deacons who betray their Pastor immediately become disqualified to remain in the office of deacon. One of the two reasons deacon ministries exist is to assist the Pastor in ministry. When this trust is violated one can be forgiven but should not be reinstated to their role as a deacon.

Deacons are often the moving force behind the removal of Pastors. This happens too often. Pastors know which Churches routinely remove their Pastors. This is not a secret. It is sad: no wonder so many Churches fail to grow. If the Pastor had some moral failing this is completely understandable. But when the removal of Pastor is over differences between a deacon and the Pastor the deacon needs to step aside and let another take his place. Churches who cut the Pastor's salary are really cutting ministry. Today, because of cell phones, a Church secretary in most Churches is unnecessary. It makes a lot more sense to have a financial secretary that answers to a Finance Chairman or the Trustees. If a Church secretary is necessary, then they should be a person known for their integrity. Church secretaries see everyone who is coming and going and has the potential to be a horrific thorn in the side of the Pastor. Some, knowing the Church secretary, refuse to come to the Church for counseling. This is a compounded issue if the Church secretary is also the wife of a deacon. The potential for harm is tremendous.

The integrity of a deacon is of the utmost importance. Separating deacons from administrative affairs of the Church frees them for ministry and protects them from any accusations concerning financial dealings associated with the Church. This is in keeping with the Biblical guidelines found in 1 Timothy. Additionally, it places them under the supervision of the local Pastor. The Pastor who is not the supervisor of the deacons, is in store for heartache. Deacons by design, according to Scripture, must be submissive to Pastoral authority. Otherwise, these deacons stand contrary to Scripture. Pastoral supervision allows the Pastor, as the under shepherd for Christ to lead in ministry. The Pastor is uniquely situated to bring a sharp focus on ministry.

Every deacon ministry is Important

Returning to Acts Chapter 6 the Apostles studied the situation and concluded that *they* were to blame for the controversy in the Jerusalem Church. The Apostles were so busy serving tables that they were neglecting prayer and the ministry of the Word of God. They had created their own problem because they were trying to do too much. Even today, some pastors are so busy with secondary tasks that they fail to spend adequate time in study and in prayer. This creates a "spiritual deficiency" in the church that makes it easy for problems to develop. Some Churches have prepared detailed job description for new Pastors. This is usually due to a perceived failure on the part of the previous Pastor. These job descriptions usually tie the hands of the Pastor. For example, requiring the Pastor to spend 20 hours each week in the office. What happens if he has three funerals that week? Or a Church family wishes for the Pastor to conduct a funeral of a long-time member who is to be buried in another state? These are just some real-life examples of how a pastoral job description can hurt ministry.

In the case of the Jerusalem Church, it became impossible for the Apostles to continue to serve tables. Look closely at their reasoning!

> **Then the twelve summoned the multitude of the disciples and said, "It is not desirable that we should leave the word of God and serve tables.**[143]

This is not to suggest that serving tables is a menial task, because *every* ministry in the church is important. But it is a matter of priorities; the Apostles were doing jobs that others could do just as well. D.L. Moody used to say that it was better to put ten men to work than to try to do the work of ten men. Certainly, it is better for the Pastor and for the church to enlist workers.[144]

It is important to realize that Deacons are assigned work rather than being left to their own devices. Deacons do many things, but there is **one thing deacons are not and that is rulers**. Deacons are servants from start to finish. When they move into the role of rulers and or administrators, their ministry suffers, and their integrity is often diminished. This is one of the dangers of a Deacon board. This implies rulership and runs counter to servanthood that Jesus praised. The whole idea of a "Deacon Board" implies authority and/or rulership. There is no Biblical basis for this concept.

It is a mistaken belief that deacons deal with the business of the Church: financial business or personnel business of the Church. In the New King James Version, the "seven" laymen were selected to tend "this

---

[143] *The New King James Version* (Nashville: Thomas Nelson, 1982), Ac 6:2.
[144] Warren W. Wiersbe, *The Bible Exposition Commentary* (Wheaton, IL: Victor Books, 1996), Ac 6:1.

business. (referring to serving tables)" Some erroneously interpret this to mean "*the* business" of the church. Of course, a congregation *may* assign to deacons additional responsibility for the financial, physical, and business affairs of the church. It is important that deacons resist this movement as it moves them from their role in ministry. But in the Jerusalem church the seven were charged with (a) peacemaking, healing the breach in the fellowship, (b) strengthening the ministry of the apostles by shielding them from criticism and relieving them of menial secondary tasks, (c) functioning as under shepherds to the congregation. These seven **were not a board of directors** running the church. They were spiritually minded servants of the congregation undergirding the preaching and teaching of the apostles.[145] The role of these men was one of the underlining factors of the explosive growth the Church of Jerusalem realized. These godly men were servants, not rulers. **If deacons are going to insist on having authority, power and prestige then let us call them what they really are: Pharisees and Sadducees.** Is this a harsh criticism? It is harsh and accurate!

Practical issues in the Family Church

This is often the source of many problems and trouble in family Churches where deacons are often related either by blood or marriage or both. Sadly, this prevents what their Church truly needs – a long term Pastor. In this instance the building or buildings and the Church Cemetery often become more important than the actual mission and ministry of the Church. When this happens, the Church becomes an edifice of man rather than a Worshiping and Praising Community devoted to God. This is what happened to the Jewish Temple at the time of Jesus. It had ceased being a place of worship and became an edifice of man. A beautiful edifice, but it no longer reflected the Glory of God.

Throughout Christian history men have tended to deify buildings and sanctify places. Fellowship often is broken by a proposal to move the

---

[145] *The Teacher's Bible Commentary*, ed. Franklin H. Paschall and Herschel H. Hobbs (Nashville: Broadman and Holman Publishers, 1972), 692-93.

church *location* or to modify or replace the physical *facility*. "God is a spirit" and he dwells not in houses of wood but in the hearts of men and in the bodies of the believers, which is the true church.[146] Pastors hear things like, "My father built this Church!" or "My grandfather cut the timber for the floors of this Church and we are not going to remove them." One Church has some beautiful stained-glass windows in what was known as the crying room in the back of the Church. Over time, the Church aged and a need for a bathroom on the main floor became a necessity. Plans were drawn up and money was donated specifically to build the bathroom. A deacon and a descendant of one of the people who donated the stained-glass window objected to putting a bathroom there. More than ten years later no bathroom was built, and the money was never used for building the bathroom, Sadly, the Churches' reputation was harmed. Incidentally, the Church never returned the money given to build the bathroom.

Typically, many become invested in a building due to its historic significance rather than to its mission and ministry. Or even a cemetery filled with dead relatives. In situations like this many begin to refer to the Church as theirs rather than God's Church. Although this may seem like a little thing it does denote over-familiarity with the Church of God and could begin a move to supplant God from the rulership of God's Church.

In Conclusion: Practical issues for little "d" deacons.

A lot of material was covered in this section. Hopefully, all of it will positively impact the Pastor and little "d" deacon's ministry in the local Church. The Constitution and bylaws are legal documents that can be changed according to the procedures of the local Church while maintaining the legality required. Unfortunately, some Churches treat these documents as holy writ.

---

[146] *The Teacher's Bible Commentary*, ed. Franklin H. Paschall and Herschel H. Hobbs (Nashville: Broadman and Holman Publishers, 1972), 693.

Regarding deacon ministry, perhaps the single most important thing a church can do is to eliminate the administrative tasks for deacons. Secondly, though not specifically addressed here is to remove any requirement concerning the number of deacons that an individual Church requires. Not all Church requires twelve deacons or even seven deacons or even one deacon. Here we can follow the leadership of the Pastor or if a need arises then the Church can address it at that time, just like they did in the Jerusalem Church, during the time of the apostles.[147] In reality most Churches have deacons ministering and serving in varying degrees. In each of these cases deacons are crucial in determining the longevity of the Pastor.

Many would likely agree that **the longevity of the Pastor is perhaps the most important factor of a successful Church**. This of course assumes the right Pastor and the right Church. It is far better for a Pastor to come to a Church with the desire to grow the Church, investing his whole life into that specific Church, than career leap from one Church to another. The primary concern of both the Pastor and the deacons must be the Church of Jesus Christ. The Church is still Jesus' Church. Too often, when conflict between deacons and the Pastor arises the Pastor begins searching for a new position. Deacons are often cited as the main reason for leaving a Church.

There is no doubt that according to Scripture the Church belongs to Christ. First and foremost, God's people are accountable to HIM. Sometimes we might say our Church, or deacons might say my Church, or the Pastor may say, when talking to another Pastor, "at my Church" we instinctively know what they mean. They mean this is the Church I go to, or I Pastor. In reality, it is Jesus' Church, and we are HIS people. Sometimes deacons, Pastors and even Church members might really mean this is "MY" Church. If that is true, then it has ceased to be God's

---

147   As of August 2018, the Church where my membership lies, is small and has no deacons. The Pastor has had a little fun with this seeing has how I am writing a book about deacons and chose to join a Church without deacons. The irony is not lost on me. I affirm I have a great Pastor. Pastors need pastors too.

Church. That was the case of the Laodicean Church in Revelation. No believer wants to be a part of a Laodicean Church. Prior to accepting any call to a local Church, the prospective Pastor must discover who does the Church belong to? Any answer, other than this is God's Church is the wrong answer. How the Pastor and the people view the local Church will define ministry. Let every prospective Pastor or church member first discover if the local Church belongs to God or to man!

Review the legal documents of the Church and examine how they impact ministry. Codify the relationship that deacons have with their pastor. For example: The Senior Pastor is the supervisor of all ministry staff including paid staff and non-paid staff, including deacons. This change will make life much easier for future pastors. Everyone needs to be accountable to someone. The Pastor is accountable to the Elders of the Church if such an office has been established and if not then the congregation. It is important to remember that the Pastor has been called of God and the congregation affirmed this calling when the local Church called their Pastor. The relationship between the Pastor and the deacons should be one of "fellow servants", however, both have a role to play, and each has his own position.

In many Churches, during business meetings, deacons have an opportunity to make motions or recommendations to the Church. These motions or recommendations should be directly connected to their role as servants, not administrators. Deacons should stay away from non-ministry related business like a Jew stayed away from lepers in Jesus' day. Like any other Church member, if they have a concern or issue, they should contact the appropriate committee and let them know of their concerns. Often people fail to contact the appropriate person to talk to, and rather than seek a resolution, spread gossip or negative comments instead of seeking to resolve the problem. Therefore, the study of what happened in the early Church in Jerusalem is so important and can provide an understanding of how to resolve Church conflict. Larger Churches would be wise to ensure that the congregation knows that individual members can directly contact committee members to share their concerns. In Churches that have elder ministry plans, then individual members could and should directly contact Church elders or the appropriate committee with their concerns. Churches commonly have committees for all kinds of things. This confuses most Church members. The fewer committees the better. Special events can have committees appointed and their tenure ends when the event is completed. This is an excellent methodology.

Before any significant change in the local Churches' policy an intensive education program needs to be developed for all congregational members: who is eligible to vote in Church business decisions. Moving from big "D" Deacons to a little "d" deacon program is an example of the importance of providing Biblical education to Church members. The soundest advice one can give: Stay close to Scripture, ensuring Scripture supports any action taken.

CHAPTER EIGHT

Practical Issues for the Local Church

NOWHERE IS THE AUTHOR OFFERING LEGAL ADVICE. ALWAYS CONSULT A LAWYER OVER LEGAL MATTERS.

C hurch constitutions and bylaws are the basic legal documents of the Local Church and as such are especially important documents and should reflect the growing issues in cultural and legal trends. If a Church must go to or be summoned by the Government, it is these documents that the Government (Judges/ Lawyers) are going to be most interested in. The next thing they will likely want to know is how faithful the Church is to its constitution and bylaws.

Next, we will examine how the Church conducts itself in relation to the Church's constitution and bylaws. It would seem reasonable that these important documents should be carefully examined every few years. In this way the local Church can protect itself from current events/trends. This is increasingly important as our nation becomes increasingly hostile to all things of God. Naturally, we should not be surprised at how the winds change from one president to another. Or what ungodly cultural or political trends develop or continue to develop in the near future. Likely, the local Church will continue to face difficult spiritual issues concerning the continued sexualization of our culture and the move to have a more European view of culture. Abortions, euthanasia, assisted government suicides, and the elimination of those that are physically impaired will continue to be issues that will be major moral issues of the coming years. The more God's people stand against these cultural trends the more hostile the government will be to believers and the more scrutiny that our legal documents will have. In countries where persecution is on the rise, at some point the Law of the Land will be increasingly used against believers. We can see this in Egypt, India, and other nations where persecution has the power of the Government behind it. In the most liberal of states, the Church is at the greatest risk.

General Warning!

A few years ago, this would not even be an issue in Evangelical circles. Transgenderism, Homosexuality, and the Gay agenda is becoming increasingly accepted by young people: so says Pew Research.[148] In Pew's introductory statement concerning the acceptance of elements of the Homosexual agenda they found the following:

> Americans' views toward those who identify as lesbian, gay, bisexual, or transgender (LGBT) have changed substantially in recent years, and a majority of U.S. adults now say homosexuality should be accepted by society. The legal landscape for LGBT people has also shifted; including through a Supreme Court decision two years ago this month that legalized same-sex marriage nationwide.[149]

Now imagine that a member of the local Church who happens to be a homosexual but keeps his private life private is nominated and voted on and confirmed as a deacon and then reveals his homosexuality. It is not difficult to imagine the media interest in such an event. Or perhaps more likely the individual is transgender and is married and a "one-woman

---

[148] Pew Research Center is a nonpartisan fact tank that informs the public about the issues, attitudes and trends shaping the world. We conduct public opinion polling, demographic research, content analysis and other data-driven social science research. We do not take policy positions. http://www.pewresearch.org/

[149] http://www.pewresearch.org/fact-tank/2017/06/13/5-key-findings-about-lgbt-americans/

man". Further imagine the local Church takes actions to remove him as a deacon. And he sues the Church for violating the constitution and bylaws regarding his dismissal. In no way is this a recommendation that every Church should put into their bylaws anti-homosexual language. The point of this exercise is to encourage Churches to closely examine their constitution and bylaws. A similar situation has occurred in one Southern Baptist Church and should be studied by Churches who view the LGBT agenda as a spiritual threat (The Ordeal and Tragedy of Binkley Baptist Church: by John L. Humber).

The above scenario can happen. In most cases, Churches have a fixed number of deacon positions, as well as term limits for both deacons and the deacon chairman. Some Churches call deacons for life but require a yearly call for the Pastor. Fortunately, the practice of a yearly call for a Pastor is increasingly growing out of favor. Because in most Evangelical Churches, Church members can make nominations from the floor; almost anyone could be voted for as a deacon, and for that matter, any officer. Examining the constitution and bylaws every few years can help protect the Church from ill-advised actions due to cultural changes or trends. The scenario above is completely fictional! However, "A Southern Baptist congregation in Chapel Hill, N.C., has become the second church to defy leaders of the 15-million-member denomination by taking a permissive stance on homosexuality."[150] This is not a recent event, but occurred in 1992! almost thirty years ago. Binkley Memorial Baptist Church voted with a narrow margin of 57% in favor. Even today it is hard to imagine that this can happen in a Southern Baptist Church. The legal protections for Churches are being eroded constantly. In Florida, Sarasota County Churches are taxed. Times are changing, and not for the better when God's people are concerned. The constitution and bylaws are important, as is following them; if the Church has these documents and does not follow them the courts may take that into consideration as well. First Century Churches suffered persecution;

---

[150] http://articles.latimes.com/1992-04-11/local/me-216 1 southern-baptist Church Stance on Gays Stirs Southern Baptists: Sexual orientation: The denomination considers a new method to remove congregations after the licensing of a homosexual for the ministry in Chapel Hill.

the Modern Church should expect nothing less. The Church must be prepared.

In the case of Binkley Memorial, the Church surrendered its moral authority and rejected the Word of God concerning the prohibition of illicit sexual choices. Some of those that push a homosexual agenda have targeted Christians before and will likely continue to do so.

How are deacons chosen?

Churches choose deacons in several ways; some are more Biblical than others. In Churches where the Bible is still held in HIGH ESTEEM, the practice of choosing deacons should follow the Biblical record as closely as possible. For most this seems reasonable, but in practice this is not always the case. For instance, the number of deacons is not a fixed number. Nowhere do we find that a specific number of deacons is required, though many Churches have used Seven or Twelve. The argument for these two numbers is amazingly simple to understand: Seven, is for the first seven deacons in the book of Acts and Twelve is the number of the apostles. But why not eleven? After all, one of the disciples was Judas. Some also suggest that twelve should be used because of the twelve patriarchs. Remember, the early Church choose Matthias, by lot, to replace Judas. So, using Twelve minus Judas would leave the original eleven plus Matthias[151] and then add Saul, who was renamed Paul, and we have thirteen as a possible number. The point here is that there is no specific number of deacons that a Church must

---

[151] NKJV Acts 1: **21** "Therefore, of these men who have accompanied us all the time that the Lord Jesus went in and out among us, **22** beginning from the baptism of John to that day when He was taken up from us, one of these must become a witness with us of His resurrection." **23** And they proposed two: Joseph called Barsabas, who was surnamed Justus, and Matthias. **24** And they prayed and said, "You, O Lord, who know the hearts of all, show which of these two You have chosen **25** to take part in this ministry and apostleship from which Judas by transgression fell, that he might go to his own place." **26** And they cast their lots, and the lot fell on Matthias. And he was numbered with the eleven apostles.

have. There is no New Testament standard regarding the total number of deacons. No standard like this exists! This can be a real problem for many small Churches where there is a limited number of eligible men to fulfill the role of deacon. In some Churches no one fulfills this role. This in no way diminishes the Church, but demonstrates harmony within most local Churches. Deacons are only a necessity when ministry demands it. Let the dictates of ministry be the deciding factor for the number of deacons needed.

The above discussion may seem out of place under the topic of: "**How is a deacon chosen?** Deacons are not essential to the Church. Prior to Acts 6 there were no deacons or anyone functioning in the role of deacon. Remember, there was a specific problem that arose that facilitated the creation of deacon ministry. If a Church is fortunate to have so few problems, they are a blessed Church and worthy of study. Such Churches, in fact, do exist: currently, Eastview of Tuscaloosa has no deacons and is a vibrant Baptist Church. This is a small Church whose people have servant hearts.

Following the completion of the New Testament, intense persecution arose against the Church, although the persecution was not universal but sporadic, it was often intense. In the days following the last of the apostles, persecution sometimes was used as a pretext to take land and possessions of Christians and sometimes used for political reasons. Whatever the cause the test was similar. The individual was asked to denounce Jesus and to either burn incense for or offer a sacrifice to Caesar. Today, we see similar persecutions against Coptic Christians in Egypt and Christians in India. These persecutions have been documented by **The Voice of the Martyrs** as well as by secular media. If it is true that persecutions are on the rise in our world then we should be aware that this has happened before and for the Christian they generally lose their jobs, ability to earn a living and are disposed of property and legal protections. As persecutions continue it will influence who is eligible to serve as a deacon or a Pastor.

> ...a decree of Saint Cornelius, in conjunction with the African Bishops, and all the Bishops throughout the world, that those who had denied the faith, might be admitted to penance, but not restored to any Priestly office.[152]

In that day it was generally understood that if one denied the faith then they were no longer eligible to serve in Ministry. The early Church understood the seriousness of the actions of those that repudiated the name of Christ Jesus. The guidelines in Acts 6 and 1 Timothy 3 are established as standards for deacons. Like Stephen, the first Christian martyr, deacons may be called upon by Christ Jesus to surrender their own lives for HIS sake. Because deacons are often the face of the local Church, it would seem likely that they would be some of the first to suffer persecution. Early in the book of Revelation believers were/are encouraged to "endure to the end!" It seems impossible to interpret this any other way, but deacons and Pastors must be willing suffer martyrdom like Stephen did in the First Century Church. Rejecting Christ disqualifies one from serving in formal ministry. Spiritual weakness is a disqualifying condition for a deacon candidate.

How, then are deacons chosen? For the purposes of this little book, the Biblical model is the only one acceptable! In the case of the Jerusalem Church, which was suffering from increasing persecution, two problems were presented: one, some widows were not being treated fairly within the local Church and two, the apostles time to study and meditate on the Word of God was being hindered.

> NKJV Acts 6: 2 **Then the twelve summoned the multitude of the disciples and said, "It is not desirable that we should leave the word of God and serve tables. ³ Therefore, brethren, seek out from among you seven men of *good* reputation, full of the Holy Spirit and wisdom, whom we may appoint over this business.**

---

[152] E. B. Pusey, Councils of the Church from the Council of Jerusalem A.D. 51, to the Council of Constantinople A.D. 381, Chiefly as to Their Constitution, but Also as to Their Objects and History (London: John Henry Parker, 1857), 64–65. Ib. fin. p. 213.

Notice the apostles, including Matthias, chose the number of men needed for this work. It would seem reasonable that Pastors are the best candidates to choose how many deacons are needed at any given time. This number likely changes as the Church prospers and grows. If a deacon has a lot of free time, perhaps only two deacons are needed. If the Church is filled with young families, the same size Church might need six deacons to do the same job. One thing is certain; these men need to have a strong testimony for Christ. They must be Scripturally sound, knowledgeable, and bold in the public sphere for the cause of Christ Jesus.

The first question then is how many deacons are needed? A fixed number is not a wise choice, as has been illustrated. The number should be able to move both up and down. The number of eligible men then needs to be determined. On this point the Scripture is not crystal clear. Holding to a high view of Scripture, two choices are available: one, men only, or two, a man and his wife form a deacon team. Remember Phoebe! And remember in 1 Timothy 3 the wives also have qualifications. Both cases have strong arguments supporting their positions. And it is up to the local Church and the local Pastor to decide who is and is not eligible to be a deacon. In today's current cultural climate where many sexual accusations are being leveled, the husband/wife deacon team will likely become more of the norm. There are stories in the Old Testament where sexual accusations were leveled at Joseph the dreamer and Daniel unjustly. Only considering practical cultural issues, when deacons are needed in Church ministry, a minimum of two deacons seems reasonable, but no maximum number can be legitimately suggested. Two deacons can go where one deacon cannot! Each deacons can support and defend his fellow deacon.

After a problem or problems have been identified and the number of deacons required is decided upon, and a plan to rectify the problems have been chosen, the next step is of a much more practical concern. The next step is clearly identified in Acts 6:

NKJV Acts 6: 5**And the saying pleased the whole multitude. And they chose Stephen, a man full of faith and the Holy Spirit, and Philip, Prochorus, Nicanor, Timon, Parmenas, and Nicolas, a proselyte from Antioch, 6 whom they set before the apostles; and when they had prayed, they laid hands on them.**

Presumably, these men were examined and held to some unstated standards that the apostle Paul later codified in First Timothy 3. What we know of Stephen and Philip, two of the seven, suggest this was so. What we know of Philip and Stephen is that they both had great courage, were used of God, were held in high esteem by others in the Church, evangelized, took their calling seriously, and were leaders in their own right; servants like Jesus called all of us to be; and men who were prepared to give everything to God. Of the first seven deacons these two are the only ones we know anything of significance about. Stephen died for his testimony and Philip witnessed across cultural boundaries. **Both were soul winners**.

In conclusion to: "How is a deacon chosen? A problem or problems are identified; the Pastor determines the number of deacons needed to resolve the problem(s), the Church chooses men meeting the qualifications of 1 Timothy 3, and the Pastor confirms the selections through prayer. Notice a lot of details are missing. The steps to nominate deacons is left unsaid in Scripture. How this is done is left to the Church.

Some form of testing is needed prior to nominating a candidate to becoming a deacon. Two forms of testing are suggested: One form of testing could be a mentoring program where the candidate deacon becomes the shadow of an effective little "d" deacon. A second form of testing would be for the Pastor to personally disciple potential deacon candidates over a period of at least one year; this testing is best left to the Pastor. Of course, a combination of the two would also be effective. In the case where both methods of testing are utilized the deacon mentor provides the practical training while the Pastor provides the Biblical training. This period of testing can and should be used to determine the candidate's spiritual maturity.

In many positions, in the general work force, a written test for potential job seekers is required. Deacon nominees could/should also have an examination. In 1 Timothy 3: 1 we read: This *is* a faithful saying: If a man desires the position of a bishop, **he desires a good work**. [153] It would seem the same should be said of potential deacons. A written examination or a written statement by deacon nominees could prove useful in selecting deacons and weeding out the candidate pool. Testing should be taken very seriously; consider the following:

> Their general character, as described in verse 8, 9, must not be taken upon loose hearsay, but must be put to the test by examination, by special testimony, by inquiry, and then, if they are ἀνέγκητοι, not accused, not open to just blame, *blameless*, **let them** be admitted to serving as deacons[154]

Please notice this is not just a group of Pastors sitting around a table asking a few questions and then voting on an individual candidate. Currently this is often the most examination that deacons have. This is a process that may last for some time. During the period of testing the following list of questions may prove helpful, as a beginning point for potential deacons that begins a season of testing.

> Tell us of your conversion experience?
>
> Have you ever given a public testimony outside of the Church? Where? When? Result?
>
> What is a deacon?
>
> What are the current deacons doing in terms of ministry?
>
> What is the purpose of a deacon?
>
> How many times have you been married? How many times has your wife been married?

---

153   *The New King James Version* (Nashville: Thomas Nelson, 1982), 1 Ti 3:1.

154   H. D. M. Spence-Jones, ed., *1 Timothy*, The Pulpit Commentary (London; New York: Funk & Wagnalls Company, 1909), 53.

What is the relationship between a deacon and his pastor?

What is the Biblical role of our Pastor?

What is the relationship between a deacon and his church?

Explain what a servant is according to the teachings of Jesus?

If a written examination is required, remember not everyone can read effectively. Reading is not a requirement for being a deacon. A written examination like this should be given early in the testing process and form a basis for discussion during the pastoral discipleship of potential deacons. Having an effective testing program is a faithful response to Scripture. This should be the goal of the Church in every decision.

Usually, questions like those listed above are asked during an oral ordination examination. And usually, they are asked the afternoon of a scheduled Ordination Service. When this occurs as is the usual practice it is almost impossible to reject a nominee. In fact, the author, in his research, did not discover a single person being refused ordination as the result of an ordination interview held prior to an ordination ceremony. An Oral interview should be the last step prior to ordination, not the **ONLY** step.

Should deacons be ordained? This should be easy, there are only two choices: yes or no. Reading this little book from the beginning, the reader should realize that this little book does not take the easy path.

For most Baptists two names stand out history that are unrivaled in the modern era: D. L Moody and Charles Haddon Spurgeon. Spurgeon was opposed to ordination and refused ordination for himself. D. L. Moody greatly admired Brother Spurgeon and followed in Spurgeon's example; neither were ordained. Speaking of ordination Brother Spurgeon gave this famous comment:

"ordination is like laying, "empty hands on empty heads""

In all honesty Spurgeon was speaking about the ordination of Pastors. But it does not seem unlikely to conclude that he felt the same thing about deacon ordination. Ultimately it is left up to the local Church. Traditionally, deacons are ordained. But like Spurgeon believed, traditions need to be closely reviewed and regularly evaluated. If an individual is doing Godly things, witnessing, and completing good works for the Church then God has already placed HIS seal upon that individual. Ordination does not change anyone. God has called or HE has not. An Ordination Certificate is merely a piece of paper showing that a Church (or a denomination) has found you worthy to minister. No one needs to be Ordained to be a minister or to do ministry.

Baptists hold firm to the idea of the "priesthood of the believer"; **no certificate is needed. This priesthood is your birthright as a Christian.**

> NKJV 1 Peter 2:4 **Coming to Him** *as to* **a living stone, rejected indeed by men, but chosen by God** *and* **precious, ⁵you also, as living stones, are being built up a spiritual house, a holy priesthood, to offer up spiritual sacrifices acceptable to God through Jesus Christ.**

Believers are a **holy priesthood,** but later Peter provides us additional information concerning our priesthood.

> NKJV 1 Peter 2:9 **But you** *are* **a chosen generation, a royal priesthood, a holy nation, His own special people, that you may proclaim the praises of Him who called you out of darkness into His marvelous light.**

All believers are a **holy royal priesthood** and **a holy nation** of Jesus. This is often expressed as the **Priesthood of Believers**. For most evangelicals this is a key doctrine; it also has roots in the Old Testament as well. For example, in outline form:

I. To proclaim God's plan to bless the nations: Genesis 12: 3

> NKJV Genesis 12:3 **I will bless those who bless you, And I will curse him who curses you; And in you all the families of the earth shall be blessed."**

II. To participate in God's Priesthood: Exodus 19: 4-6

NKJV Exodus 19: 5 **Now therefore, if you will indeed obey My voice and keep My covenant, then you shall be a special treasure to Me above all people; for all the earth is Mine. ⁶ And you shall be to Me a kingdom of priests and a holy nation.' These are the words which you shall speak to the children of Israel."**

III. God's purpose is to bless all the Nations: Psalm 67

NKJV Psalm 67: 1 **God be merciful to us and bless us, *And* cause His face to shine upon us, Selah**

²That Your way may be known on earth, Your salvation among all nations.

³Let the peoples praise You, O God; Let all the peoples praise You.

⁴Oh, let the nations be glad and sing for joy! For You shall judge the people righteously And govern the nations on earth. Selah

⁵Let the peoples praise You, O God; Let all the peoples praise You.

⁶*Then* the earth shall yield her increase; God, our own God, shall bless us.

⁷God shall bless us, And all the ends of the earth shall fear Him.[155]

The doctrine of the Priesthood of the believers is only directly represented in 1 Peter but its roots reach deep into the Old Testament. The Jewish people, as the Apple of God's eye, were to be a world-wide missionary people. Israel rejected Jesus and failed in this missionary call. The

---

[155] *The New King James Version* (Nashville: Thomas Nelson, 1982), Ps 67:1–7.

Church is now God's instrument in the World. But God is not through with Israel (that is another book for another day). The best days of Israel are still before them, especially in the Millennial Kingdom. Before deacons were deacons, they held membership in the **Royal Priesthood of God** and after becoming a deacon **they are still members of God's Holy Priesthood**. Nothing changed except the deacon has a piece of paper stating he is a deacon. Should deacons be ordained? Ordained or not, they are still deacons if chosen to do a specific ministry by the Church.

What is the <u>Holy Royal Priesthood</u> to do?

> "A holy priesthood offers up spiritual sacrifices, acceptable to God by Jesus Christ". Another picture which this epistle gives to us is that of a holy priesthood. All believers are living stones. All believers are priests. We are a holy priesthood, and later Peter calls it a royal priesthood. As priests we are to offer up spiritual sacrifices, acceptable to God in Jesus Christ. Praise to God is such a spiritual sacrifice. . . . And then, you can offer yourself to God. That is a spiritual sacrifice.[156]

Since we are already a part of the Priesthood why do we have need of ordination? Spurgeon makes an impassioned plea opposing ordination. And though he was a Baptist, other Baptists disagreed and supported ordination. This should not be surprising! Every Baptist Church is an independent Church, coming together for missions and other common issues.

In the past, early Baptists steered away from using the word "ordination", fearing it would link them to the Catholic Pope. This was a reaction to the Catholic claim that the apostolic torch was passed from the apostle Peter down through the long line of Popes (including the bad ones) to the present day; Baptists totally rejected and still reject the Roman Catholic idea of ordination tradition. The doctrine of the Priesthood

---

[156] J. Vernon McGee, *Thru the Bible Commentary: The Epistles (1 Peter)*, electronic ed., vol. 54 (Nashville: Thomas Nelson, 1991), 50–51.

of the Believer is a clear and correct reaction against Roman Catholic apostolic ascension. This doctrine's emphasis is directed to the "spiritual right" of the individual to be used of God rather than a central Christian leader to act as spiritual guide for the world. Yet ordination still existed in some form, even in the early days of Baptist History.

> 'Baptist churches, governed by congregational policy as dictated by the equal status of each baptized member, chose and authorized congregational leaders not as lords over them, but as servant ministers. Divine authority in Baptist beginnings did not trickle down from ordained clergy to the common Christian but flowed upward through the members of the congregation to its chosen leaders. The very term ordination was avoided for several decades in the two original Baptist groups, Generals and Particulars, in favour of terms such as '**set apart,' 'called,' and 'appointed**."[157]

The preferred terminology of many rural churches still remains as '**set apart,' 'called,' and 'appointed.** An additional term that that still retains some appeal is "anointed for service". Although ordination was not used it amounted to the same thing in practice. Some Churches may still be hesitant to use the word "ordination" although the certificate issued to Pastors and deacons is entitled "ordination certificate". This is little more than wordplay and is not an argument either for or against ordination.

Ordination does serve some purposes. Ordination is a confirmation of at least one Church testifying for an individual's character. This is more important for a Pastor as some seminaries give a discount for tuition. The United States Military requires either ordination or some similar declaration before one can become a Military Chaplain. In the case of ordination for a Military Chaplain, it acts as a professional declaration of the fitness of the ordained. Interestingly, there are exemptions for some religious groups. For the world in which ordination is a needed

---

[157] WM Lloyd Allen, The Meaning of Ordination, 2000. Retrieved from http:// www.baptisthistory.org/contissues/allen.htm on 05/03/15

requirement, especially for Chaplains and Pastors in these cases, ordination provides a kind of professional recognition.

There is zero evidence in Acts 6 or 1 Timothy 3 that deacons were ordained. This does not mean that they were not ordained but that there is no evidence that they were. It is the common **modern day tradition** among evangelicals that deacons are ordained. The roots of this in America goes back to Colleges, Universities and Seminaries such as Harvard and Princeton. And to Episcopalism and Presbyterianism and other forms of liturgical Churches often called High Churches. Certainly, the installation of deacons should be marked by a religious occasion. Usually this is done in the afternoon following the examination of deacon candidates. The reason for this is so active Pastors can be present during both the examination and installation service for the new deacons. These Pastors can then publicly affirm their support of the new deacons by the laying on of hands and return to their own Churches. In the case of many Churches, a timeline exists that makes it almost **impossible not to select** a deacon once he enters the nominating process regardless of how the interview goes! Where is the testing of deacons in modern evangelical Churches? Testing is a basic requirement for any deacon selection.

With an abbreviated examination period, with little or no testing, with little or no examination and with little or no discipleship, what kind of deacons can we expect to have in our Churches? Even the finest candidate, with the most excellent credentials and such wonderful beginnings will have a hard time navigating the course to become an effective deacon. The Biblical process is important; if we take seriously the Biblical mandate concerning deacon ministry, then testing, watching, and discipleship will play a more important role in preparing men of God to be deacons.

In the case of ordination for deacons this is a tradition of men. Traditions within the Church are not always bad! But traditions like the Church's bylaws and constitutions should be reviewed every few years. Denominations that are top down driven like Presbyterians, Methodists, and others; Ordinations may be helpful, for the Ordination comes from the Denomination. For independent Churches, Baptist, and other evangelical Churches, ordination especially for Deacons is not necessary. The question arises, **"Does the Ordination of Deacons"** harm the local Church? There is no simple answer to this question! Recently, a Church in Birmingham Alabama closed its doors and handed over the keys to the building to an African American Congregation. Now deacons from the Church that closed its doors go to another Church. And based on their credentials they are still ordained deacons. Now the new Church should wonder if they were good or bad deacons. How would you know? How could you find out? Do you care? **This highlights the problem of ordaining deacons for life!** If a local Church decides to ordain or not to ordain, that is the business of that local Church! The recommendation of the author is that Ordination, if used, should have a term limit. Ordain but only for the life of the Deacon term which is often three years or less; perhaps it should be less, more like eighteen months. The job of a Deacon is a hard job. It can be stressful, and every deacon is on call 24 hours a day 7 days a week. Certainly, wise deacons have a system of who is on call but when an emergency comes all hands on deck is a job requirement. Deacon term limits is a wise requirement established by the Church. And the recommendation here is that the Ordination Certificate should be limited to that term.

IN CONCLUSION CONCERNING: Should deacons be ordained? The answer is not just an easy yes or no. Biblical evidence does not exist concerning ordination of deacons. The Scriptures are silent on this point. We have in the Old Testament where kings and priests are anointed for their role in Israel, but deacons are not kings and priests. But it is equally clear that some kind of recognition and some kind of installation service should be performed as it was done in the Jerusalem Church. In the case of Jerusalem: prayer, praise and rejoicing were key components of that first deacon service. This is an excellent model. And though these first seven deacons were prayed over, and hands were laid upon them there is no evidence that was an ordination service. This was much more like a commissioning service for missionaries. The Seven were commissioned to serve widows and protect the apostles' study and prayer time. Again, no evidence of ordination can be found in Acts 6 or 1 Timothy 3 for deacons. But if a Church decides to ordain deacons, then the following suggestions are offered.

Practical suggestions for ordination.

1. If a Church elects to ordain deacons let them closely follow the Biblical mandate of testing. It is recommended that this process should take a year to complete.
2. Celebrate deacon's beginning ministry each time a deacon begins a new term of service.
3. Let the Ordination Certificate have a beginning and an ending date.
4. Each time a new deacon (including someone who was once a deacon and rotated out of service) is chosen to set aside a time for the Pastor to lead a weekend Bible study focusing on deacon ministry (Friday night, Saturday morning or a Saturday retreat). This would be a great time for deacons to testify about deacon ministry and should include all current deacons as well as the new deacons. Invite deacons from other Churches. And focus on the Scripture about what a deacon should be doing.
5. Deacons must hold each other accountable; if the Pastor must do this then the deacons have failed in one of their most important duties.
6. Deacons must be ministry driven with well-defined assigned ministries.
7. Deacons must submit to Pastoral authority or they should resign privately.
8. Deacons are fellow ministers and as such should receive no financial benefit of any Church service.
9. Failure to be engaged in ministry should be reason enough for that deacon to resign. This should be demanded by the other deacons to protect deacons' ethical standards and accountability.
10. Celebrate deacon ministry often in worship settings.

When a Church ordains anyone; that Church is making a statement about that Minister: be he a Pastor, minister of music, youth leader or a deacon! Ordination is the official stamp of approval of the local Church. No wonder character and integrity are so important! Once ordained that Ordination Certificate goes with the Ordained individual. He may be a good or a bad minister, but his name and the name of the Church are forever linked. Let ordination for deacons be for a set season limited to their term in service.

In 2018 a rash of allegations became public about ordained ministers sexually abusing children. While it was predominately Catholic priests, other denominations were not left unscathed. Ordination is taken too lightly by Churches, Pastors, denominations, and congregational members. Ordination is serious business. And because of this **The Church must not be casual about ordination**. Every bad player that is ordained is an evil mark against the Church of God. The Church is filled with sinners of every description; every believer is also a sinner, though a forgiven one. Because the local Church has saints and sinners alike, hypocrites exist in the Church. This should not be a surprise for any believer, but this illustrates how important it is to choose the right people for service. Imagine how a Church would feel if one of the people it ordained engaged in immoral activities. **Let the Church be guarded about who it will ordain or approve for service. The best guarantee is to have a rigorous test and probation process.**

Should every church have a deacon? The simple answer is no. This has been discussed before and bears reinforcing. Thinking again of Acts 6: deacon ministry came about for two specific reasons; some widows were being treated unfairly and the time for the Apostles to study and meditate on the Word of God was negatively impacted. If a local Church does not have issues that impact negatively on the Pastor's ability to study and meditate on the Word of God, then there is no need for deacons. In the case of the Jerusalem Church, ministering to widows was taking too much time from studying and meditating on Scripture, this is the essential benefit and ministry for deacon. And these early deacons were assigned to help the apostles in certain **Specified** (feeding widows) **ministries.**

The problem or problems could be anything that affects, hinders, or impedes ministry. Orphans or homelessness ministries could have been the problem, or any number of intensive ministries. Deacons help lighten the ministry load of Pastors, allowing Pastors to focus on the Ministry of the Word; their key purpose. **This is really the primary mission of deacons**. The Church members should take care of all the other issues touching the Church. Cutting the grass at the Church does not require a deacon to do. Opening the doors to the Church is not a deacon's ministry nor should ushering be one. A Church is not required to have any deacons and **NO** deacons is really a testimony to the harmony of the local Church. Yet, all too often, these are the kinds of things many deacons do and consider them ministry. The Church, primarily from the pulpit, should be reminding all believers of their responsibility to the local Church and to God's universal Church. Church members need to be equipped to be good Church members, not just **pew sitters**! Is it possible that one reason for some of the qualifications of deacons, such as: **holding the mystery of the faith with a pure conscience**; is so that they too, along with the Pastor assist in equipping the Church to greater activity? Discipleship was at one point, key in **Evangelical life**. Now it seems to be out of favor. And because it is, Pastors have a much greater need to personally disciple deacons. Jesus did this with HIS disciples and they changed the world. Remember, when the first deacons began to minister to the Christian women of Jerusalem, dramatic growth was the result. Discipleship is never a wasted effort.

God uses us all to accomplish HIS purposes. All believers are called to be servants for God's glory. Not just Pastors, ministers, or deacons. Jesus should be our example for ministry! We can ask ourselves: "What kind of ministry did Jesus do?"

> **Jesus taught, in the temple, in the street and privately with HIS disciples.**
> This is called ministry of the Word!

Jesus fed the hungry.
> Feeding ministry.

Jesus healed the Sick
> Ministry to the ill.

NKJV Matthew 25: 43 **I was a stranger and you did not take Me in, naked and you did not clothe Me, sick and in prison and you did not visit Me.'**

Ministry according to Jesus: Hospitality, clothing, Home and Hospital visitation; Prison ministries.

Evangelism ministries and apologetic ministries and Tract Ministries! There are more ministries of the Word and are different from the ministry of the hands – both are Biblical and important!

Deacons can protect the Pastor's time for both study of the Word and the Pastor's private family time as well.

> It is far better for a deacon to act on the Pastor's behalf when the congregation makes unreasonable demands on the Pastor's time. And deacons are in the best position to remind the Pastor that he needs to spend more time in study and/or with his family.

In general terms ministries are activities that focus on people. Benevolence, transportation, and home bound ministries are people driven and people focused. Counting the offering, ushering, assisting at the Lord's Table are more focused on convivience or service for efficient operations of the Church. Again, generally we have a division of administrative functions and ministry. A Church secretary is an administrator, a chairperson is an administrator, kitchen manager is also an administrator. While the Pastor may have some administrative duties, his primary focus is The Word of God. Certainly, he leads in funerals and weddings and visits the hospital; these all represent ministry either in proclamation of God's word or sharing comfort from the Word of God. The same can be said of the Youth Pastor, Minister of Education (Which has a lot of administrative duties) and other specialized ministry staff.

A South Korean deacon story (as told to the author).

There is story that was shared with the author, while he was stationed in South Korea, as an Army Chaplain.

> It was the custom of this Church that the deacons supplied all the needs of the Pastor and his family. While the offerings and tithes of the Church took care of the all the concerns of the Church, such as power, water, supplies, Sunday School material, Bibles, and tracts and all the other things necessary to care for the Church's many ministries. A terrible accident occurred, and the Pastor's children and wife were killed in an automobile accident. As anyone can imagine, the Pastor suffered greatly at the loss of his young family and the congregation grieved with their Pastor. Time passed, and the Pastor resumed his duties and things began to return to normal. After a while, the congregation noticed that their Pastor was dressing more and more shabbily week after week. Unknown to the Pastor, the congregation called the deacons and berated and shamed them because they were failing the Pastor and the Congregation due to their lack of providing for their Pastor. The South Korean cultural prohibitions did not allow a culturally acceptable way for the deacons to defend themselves. So, the deacons mounted no defense. The deacons responded by taking their Pastor shopping and bought him a new wardrobe.
>
> For a while, things returned to normal. The Pastor was back in style again. The Congregation was pleased with their deacons. And all seemed fine, for a while. Six months to a year passed and again the Pastor began to dress more and more shabbily. Again, the congregation called the deacons before them: berated them, threatened them with dismissal and shamed them to action. In all fairness to the deacons, they knew they were innocent; again,

cultural restrictions prohibited any defense. The only option was to confront their Pastor. This was difficult as a Pastor in Korea is of the highest status; Pastors are greatly respected and honored. A Pastor, in Korea, is viewed much more like an Old Testament Prophet than the way most congregations view their Pastor in the United States. Nevertheless, they confront their Pastor, violating cultural norms. The Pastor responds to the deacons by saying:

(paraphrased by the author) Now that I no longer have a family my needs are much less. And I have become more aware of the needs in our community. Now I can respond immediately to any need. If I see a man in need of shoes, I trade shoes with him. If I see one who needs a coat, I give him mine. If I see one who is hungry, I feed him. No need is so small that I cannot respond. All of this is possible because you take care of me so well".

The deacons were caught between the proverbial "rock and a hard place". On one hand these deacons recognized they had a humble man of God as their Pastor who mirrored Jesus' teachings in a remarkable way. A Pastor such as this is a rare treasure, and it was impossible to rebuke their Pastor for his humility and love for the poor and needy as Jesus taught us all. The deacons, under pressure from the congregation had to do something! Their response was as simple as it was elegant. The deacons asked the Pastor to set aside his clothing for his ministerial duties and limit the use of them to Worship services and Church functions and the deacons would supply him with the necessary clothing to give to the poor and needy he encountered. This Pastor was satisfied because he could continue ministering to the poor and needy. The deacons were relieved that the congregation no longer would be publicly shamming them. And as far as the congregation was concerned their rebuke was taken seriously and their Pastor was once again being cared for properly.

This Korean Church is unique, in my understanding. Furthermore, this was not a big Church. The deacons in this Church took care of their Pastor, empowered their Pastor's zeal to care for the poor and needy. They did this privately and discreetly. The deacons acted as true servants to their congregation and to their Pastor. Even though the Pastor unknowingly embarrassed his deacons, the deacons (to their great credit) did not throw their Pastor under the bus. Their concern was to care for their Pastor, privately and discreetly. In all of this they continued to respect and hold their Pastor in high esteem.

The purpose of telling the story of this unique Korean Church is not to encourage Churches to model their organization in this manner, but rather to show how deacons can care for their Pastors in a discreet and respectful manner. **If a Church never learns of single conversation between a Pastor and his deacons that would be a good thing!!!!** Confidentiality is crucial to maintaining a healthy Pastor-deacon relationship. Little "d" deacons love their Pastor and are discreet and respectful of the Church they attend. These actions will benefit the local congregation and God will be glorified in it.

CONCLUSION

The Pastor and the deacons need to have a level of confidentiality that makes the **FBI** look silly. Pastors and deacons often know a great deal about a lot of people. Being able to keep a confidence is crucial to maintaining effective ministries. And this is doubly important in the relationship between a Pastor and deacons. Pastors must be able to trust their deacons to be faithful in ministry. And deacons must be able to trust their Pastor to be faithful to the Word of God. A Pastor must be a faithful under shepherd of Christ. Let him be faithful and let the deacon trust him enough to follow him in ministry.

One final note for this section. Little " d" deacons will be highly available to all the people in the Church. As a result, they will often be the first to hear of any gossip about the Pastor and may then be the first to call out this destructive sin.

A final word about Ordination for deacons

Every practical Issue that might arise cannot possibly be covered in such a small book. Feel free to reach out to the author and tell more stories and share more practical suggestions. However, all the issues covered in this little book come from real life experiences. Some of these were and are still very painful. Others are joyful memories and still brings smiles. The important take away, is to always be firmly rooted in Scripture. Separate any crisis from the emotional pain and refocus it in Scripture, let Scripture shine its light on the crisis at hand.

Eliminating Ordination for deacons will be a difficult hurdle. But eliminating ordination or limiting it to a period of the term for an active deacon will help focus deacon ministry to ministry and diminish the idea of deacon as some kind of secular title. It may not be easy. Change is not easy. If it does not go well just blame it on the author.

Doing the work of a little "d" deacon is stressful and difficult if it is focused on ministry. If it is done right. Weekly visits to a hospice care unit are heart breaking. It is a heavy ministry. But the benefits are staggering. It benefits the professional caregivers, it opens up other opportunities for ministry, but most of all it blesses the servant of God. Here little "d" deacons can excel. They are often the only visitor some of the hospice patients will ever see. An eternal difference can be made here.

Almost every practical issue is a spiritual matter! Every deacon ministry is a spiritual matter, if done for God's glory. This is why it is so very crucial that the local Church chooses men of integrity with a willingness to work! Little "d" deacon ministry is a high calling fulfilling a great need within many of our Churches.

CHAPTER NINE

Other Words

The local Church is filled with imperfect people. This includes the Pastor, the staff, deacons, and every member. No one deserves to be placed on a pedestal, especially not in a local Church. One day Jesus will come for HIS Church and we will realize our Heavenly inheritance. Until then, we are to work for HIS Kingdom. This includes every single believer. All believers have this in common, including Pastors and deacons. No one is exempt! Pastors and deacons are called upon to do more, this is reasonable! Pastors and deacons are not "pew sitters" who meet once a month to discuss the business of the Church. In fact, if they are discussing business then they are likely failing to do Kingdom work and instead are working outside the authority of Scripture. The Church's constitution and the Church's bylaws may give deacons administrative duties and/or responsibilities, but this runs counter to Scripture. The local Church, no matter how well-meaning, is struggling on very thin ice when it chooses to initiate policies that run in opposition to Scripture. The role of both deacons and Pastors is ministry, while some administrative duties may be required, this should **not be** their sole or primary function.

In the book of Revelation, Jesus calls upon HIS people to endure until the end. We are called to have patience. We are called to testify of HIM despite the threat of imprisonment, death or worse. We are called to love HIM above all else and if necessary, we are called to die for HIM. In Africa and Asia this is a reality. India and Indonesia are stepping up persecutions, usually in the form of the Government standing by while radical Islamists or radical Hindus attack believers. In the United Sates many local governments are becoming increasingly hostile to Christians, especially in California, Oregon, and Washington. Democrats are formally opposed to core Christian beliefs: including, life, morality, and the free exercise of Worship and proclamation. Persecution is coming, it is just a matter of time and the right circumstances for persecution to begin in earnest here. We should study history and realize how persecution erupted in Nazi Germany by targeting Jews. Likely it will happen in a similar way here; in the United States anti – Semitism and anti - Christianity sentiments are rising. In May 2019, the New York Times (internet division) posted anti -Semitic cartoons involving the President of the United States and the Prime Minister of Israel. One thing is certain; anti – Semitism rises slowly. If not checked, as in Nazi Germany, other groups will also be targeted. History confirms that when hate is tolerated against one group, soon other groups will be targeted as well. History assures us of this fact.

In this current age, little "d" deacons are becoming increasingly crucial to our local Churches. They are the faces of the local Church. Their faithfulness and integrity will be severely tested in the coming years. This is not just a claim out of the blue! This is how the world is trending. Hostility comes first. We are already in this stage in the United States. Next comes government indifference to the plight of Christian citizens: some parts of the United States and some local governments have already reached this stage, especially in California, Colorado and Sarasota, Florida. The media is also increasingly hostile to Christianity and Christian practices, including morality. The media is already dehumanizing Evangelicals. History tells us that the media has the power to inflame the people and we can see how this has been carried out in recent years. Many witnessed this during the Obama years as riots destroyed private businesses. In some cities, the police stood by and allowed rampant vandalism to flourish and go unchecked. As the government grows indifferent to the cries of believers, more hostility will develop and increase in intensity toward the Church. The world hated Jesus; we should expect the world will become increasingly hostile for believers.

In Nazi Germany, the attacks on the Jews did not happen all at once. It began slowly and ended with millions being murdered. Even in the closing days of World War II the death camps continued to operate at ever increasing efficiency. This began with only one election.

United States citizens can see how one election can change so much, and usually not for the better. But what does this mean for the Church? The Church can expect that persecution and opposition to the Church will continue to grow. Looking at how our nation is moving we can reasonably expect that we are closer to the day Jesus Christ will return. The time for public proclamation of the Gospel is now! The time for the Church to seriously re-examine its purpose – IS NOW. NOW is the time for God's people to cry out to God for Revival. Let the little "d" deacons rise up and call for a renewed respect for Scripture, a renewed return to doctrinal teaching and a renewed interest in soul winning. To rise and call for Revival, a reviving of God's people. To rise and renew to themselves a commitment to be Jerusalem-style deacons and to insist their Pastor stays focused on Scripture, meditates, and prays, so that he might feed his people with the deep things of Christ Jesus.

Finally, let us all prepare for the coming of Lord Jesus, that we might not be ashamed at HIS coming. Let us be found witnessing and proclaiming Jesus. Little "d" deacons are in a unique position to make this happen. Be encouraged, be faithful to Scripture and be faithful to the example of Philip and Stephen. This will be pleasing to our Lord Jesus Christ. Let us unite in prayer:

Heavenly Father,
    Raise up Your people to select men who are found
    acceptable to You.
    Men of Faith
    Men of passion
    Men of Boldness
    To serve as deacons.

May they fulfill their office well, protecting the Pastor's time of study and prayer, serving the needy of the Church with an eye always on the Cross.

Protect and guide them as the world rushes to the last days.

In Jesus Name we unite in prayer.

Final comments, from the heart of the Author.

This is my personal appeal.

I am nothing. But I do believe I have a message to share.

Friends, Jesus must be our focus. Let us endeavor to be found worthy of HIS service.

This little book was not designed to hurt anyone in anyway nor to shame anyone or any of God's Churches. But anyone who pays even casual attention to God's Churches can see the Church is under increasing pressure to bow to new and radical cultural norms. We are called to be a PURE PEOPLE. To give up Bible based doctrine in order not to offend any is a tragedy of immense proportion. Churches are under attack to cave to the basest and most immoral elements of our society. The Church is being forced out of the Public Square and told to keep our Church thinking inside the Church. The call to redeem the souls of our fellow citizens has been labeled as intolerant and divisive. While Islam is portrayed as a Religion of Victims. The adherents of Islam find their religious leaders increasingly hostile to other peace-loving societies. No one is claiming all Muslims are radicals. Yet who can honestly deny that many adherents to Islam are engaging in hideous acts: such as, beheadings, forced marriages, sex trafficking, child marriages and slavery. Again, not all Muslims are engaged in such activities, but one thing is certain: all Muslims need Jesus! Let us join with Jesus and pray that we may be used of God to proclaim the Gospel of Jesus Christ to our world.

There is some good news! More Muslims are coming to Jesus today than at any other point in Human History. God is still at work, in every nation and in every people.

Ask missionaries, what is God doing in our world? Listen to their testimony. Support them.

Brothers and Sisters in Christ Jesus, I am praying for revival for our Churches and for our Nation, join with me please as we seek to be good stewards of the Gospel that has been entrusted to us. Let us be faithful in proclaiming the Gospel and fulfilling the great commission.

I passionately believe that our deacons can ignite a National Revival for Christ. Little "d" deacons stand up for Christ Jesus.

Deacons, protect your Pastor and be on guard for your Pastor. Be ready to denounce the sin of Gossip. All godly deacons know who is the "author of lies"!

APPENDIX

N OTE FROM THE AUTHOR: The following did not fit with the design and purpose of this little "d" deacon book. It is included here for a quick overview of the only two deacons in the Bible that we know something about. It is my hope that this will be a helpful overview of two outstanding deacon examples.

The Author,
Brother Jerry.

Notice the similar wording about Philip and Stephen.

NKJV Acts 6:8**And Stephen, full of faith and power, did great wonders and signs among the people.**

These signs and wonders testified of the power of God that motivated their faith and confirmed their witnesses. These two men should be examined closely by anyone desiring the office of deacon or who serves as a deacon. Both Philip and Stephen are obviously highly regarded and show a close relationship to the Apostles as well. Clearly the Apostles did not believe that the deacons were usurping their authority, rather they seem to be regarded as partners in ministry. This is a key concept in an understanding of these early deacons.

Both men, Stephen and Philip, were empowered and encouraged by the Holy Spirit, but their submission to God's leadership should not be discounted. These men faced extreme opposition and for Stephen it claimed his life. In today's world such extreme opposition is limited to heavily Muslim population areas or areas controlled by communism or socialism. The United States is relatively safe from such persecutions (right now), although the public square is increasingly hostile to the name of God. Why then are so few deacons bold for Christ? Perhaps others have had better experiences.

Philip fled to Samaria, apparently not to hide from persecution but to preach the Gospel of Jesus Christ. His ministry was fruitful and greatly used by God to proclaim the Gospel as evidenced by the miracles and signs that confirmed his ministry. Then he was plucked from this fruitful ministry and sent to one lonely man in a distant desert. Look at how great God's concern is for even a single individual.

> NKJV Acts 8:26**Now an angel of the Lord spoke to Philip, saying, "Arise and go toward the south along the road which goes down from Jerusalem to Gaza." This is desert.**

The angel of Acts 8: 26 is not Jesus, nevertheless, the angel clearly represents the Lord's interest. Philip's obedience is clear, direct, and prompt following the angel's command.

> 27**So he arose and went. And behold, a man of Ethiopia, a eunuch of great authority under Candace the queen of the Ethiopians158, who had charge of all her treasury, and had come to Jerusalem to worship,**

---

158 "Ethiopia" here refers not to modern-day Ethiopia but to ancient Nubia, the region from Aswan in southern Egypt to Khartoum, Sudan. Candace was a title given to the queen mother, as Pharaoh was used of the king of Egypt. Governmental power rested in the hands of Candace, for the royal son, worshiped as an offspring of the sun, was therefore above such mundane activities as ruling over a nation. Rulership was therefore vested with the queen mother. The fact that **this** eunuch **had gone to Jerusalem to worship** is interesting. The Law prohibited eunuchs from entering the Lord's assembly (Deuteronomy 23:1). However, Isaiah 56:3-5 predicts great blessing for eunuchs in the Millennial Age. Evidently this eunuch was a worshiper of Yahweh though not a full-fledged Jewish proselyte.

Acts 8: 28-30. The eunuch's wealth is revealed in the simple description **sitting in his chariot.** As this finance officer was riding, he was **reading** from **the Book of Isaiah.** Since it was customary to read aloud, **Philip** could have easily **heard the** portion of Scripture the eunuch was **reading** (verse 30). Interestingly **Philip** was guided first by an angel and then later with

In Philippians, the reader will discover Christians are found even in the household of Caesar.

NKJV Philippians 4: 22**All the saints greet you, but especially those who are of Caesar's household.**

In Acts 8 the reader sees how a Christian is planted in the household of Candace, a foreign power almost rivaling Roman influence. God continues to find a way to expand the Church reaching even into Africa.

[28]was returning. And sitting in his chariot, he was reading Isaiah the prophet.

The book of Isaiah is likely the most opened book of the Old Testament in Christian Churches. The Christmas story would be forever incomplete without Isaiah's prophecies.

> He was a citizen of Ethiopia, but he had come to Jerusalem to worship; likely he was a Jewish proselyte. He had just been to Jerusalem, the center of the Jewish religion and although Judaism was the God-given religion, he was leaving the city still in the dark. He was found reading the prophet Isaiah, but he was not understanding what he was reading.[159]

Not only is the Christmas story incomplete without Isaiah so is the Crucifixion story. The angel of the Lord commands Philip to travel south, the Spirit of God directs Philip to chase after a chariot and it should surprise no one that the scroll should be opened and read precisely timed to coincide with Philip's arrival. God had showed up before Philip started running. The Spirit of God planned, executed, and provided an opportunity to a single individual to come to know Jesus

---

his on intuition (verse 26) and then by **the** Holy **Spirit** (verse 29). John F. Walvoord, Roy B. Zuck and Dallas Theological Seminary, *The Bible Knowledge Commentary: An Exposition of the Scriptures* (Wheaton, IL: Victor Books, 1985), Acts 8:27–30.

[159] J. Vernon McGee, *Thru the Bible Commentary*, electronic ed. (Nashville: Thomas Nelson, 1997), Ac 8:28.

as Savior and Lord. Jesus cares for the individual as HE cares for great Nations. No one is exempt from the loving care of Jesus.

One of the first Deacons was the first martyr and now a second deacon becomes the first to lead a gentile to a saving knowledge of Jesus Christ.

> **²⁹Then the Spirit said to Philip, "Go near and overtake this chariot."**

Accidents do not happen in the will of God. Apparently, circumstances are used of God and created by God to arouse men and women to action.

> **³⁰So Philip ran to him, and heard him reading the prophet Isaiah, and said, "Do you understand what you are reading?"**

> **³¹And he said, "How can I, unless someone guides me?" And he asked Philip to come up and sit with him.**

Philip's submissive spirit to the leadership of the Holy Spirit was recognized as demonstrated in his selection as a deacon. Perhaps his close association with the Apostles and Stephen provided boldness to question a stranger. Whatever the reason that moved Philip to be available and to ask his question, if: it is the angel, the Spirit of God, or connections to godly men - Philip asked the perfect question!

What a great question! It is possible to read Scripture and not clearly see its intent. The Spirit is directing Philip to a "divine appointment" which will:

1. show a new age has dawned
2. give a powerful witness to another people group[160]

---

[160] Robert James Utley, vol. Volume 3B, *Luke the Historian: The Book of Acts*, Study Guide Commentary Series (Marshall, TX: Bible Lessons International, 2003), 117.

The firsts associated with the initial selection of "the seven" would be remarkable outside of the realm of the supernatural. God worked together what lesser men would call coincidences, but believers would easily call it a miracle.

Philip had no doubt about the Messianic meaning, and he knew that Jesus was the Messiah. There are scholars who do not find Jesus in the Old Testament at all, but Jesus did (Luke 24:27) as Philip does here.

Scientific study of the Old Testament (historical research) misses its mark if it fails to find Christ the Center of all history. The knowledge of the individual prophet is not always clear, but future events often throw a backward light that illumines it all (I Peter 1:11 and following; II Peter 1:19–21).[161]

Philip seized the opportunity and witnessed of Christ Jesus.

> [32] **The place in the Scripture which he read was this:**
>
> **"He was led as a sheep to the slaughter;**
>
> *And as a lamb before its shearer is silent, So He opened not His mouth.*
>
> [33] *In His humiliation His* **justice was taken away,** *And who will declare His generation?*
>
> **For His life is taken from the earth."**
>
> [34]**So the eunuch**[162] **answered Philip and said, "I ask you, of whom does the prophet say this, of himself or of some other man?"**

---

[161] A.T. Robertson, *Word Pictures in the New Testament* (Nashville, TN: Broadman Press, 1933), Ac 8:35.

[162] The term "official" is literally the term "eunuch." However, it is uncertain whether he was a physical eunuch or simply an official at court (derived meaning). In the Old Testament, Potiphar is called a eunuch and yet he is

³⁵Then Philip opened his mouth, and beginning at this Scripture, preached Jesus to him.

³⁶Now as they went down the road, they came to some water. And the eunuch said, "See, *here is* water. What hinders me from being baptized?"

³⁷Then Philip said, "If you believe with all your heart, you may." And he answered and said, "I believe that Jesus Christ is the Son of God."

³⁸So he commanded the chariot to stand still. And both Philip and the eunuch went down into the water, and he baptized him.

Many events and personalities lead up to the events that brought Philip to the desert all within the perview of the Holy Spirit. To think of the events that came together including the timing of Philip's arrival the speed of the chariot and the availability of water all that worked for the glory of God can only be described as many miracles strung together like lights on a string.

³⁹Now when they came up out of the water, the Spirit of the Lord caught Philip away, so that the eunuch saw him no more; and he went on his way rejoicing.

⁴⁰But Philip was found at Azotus. And passing through, he preached in all the cities till he came to Caesarea.

Following the eunuch's Baptism Philip was translated to Azotus and preached all the way to Caesarea. The time elapsed is unknown between Acts 8 and Acts 21.

---

married (compare Gen. 39:1). Robert James Utley, vol. Volume 3B, *Luke the Historian: The Book of Acts*, Study Guide Commentary Series (Marshall, TX: Bible Lessons International, 2003), 117.

^{Acts 21:8}**On the next *day* we who were Paul's companions departed and came to Caesarea, and entered the house of Philip the evangelist, who was *one* of the seven, and stayed with him. ⁹Now this man had four virgin daughters who prophesied.**

Philip must have been a remarkable man to have conversations with an angel and the Spirit of God. He travelled supernaturally, began foreign missions, ministered to the poor and received a title—**evangelist**. Now, here is a title worth having. The Spirit of God was also at work within his own household. What kind of stories must he have shared with the Apostle Paul?

> **"had four virgin daughters...prophetesses"** We need to rethink our position on women in leadership positions (cf. Joel 2:28–32; Acts 2:16–21) in the church based on all New Testament evidence. See Special Topic: Women in the Bible at 2:17. The issue is ambiguous. Church tradition says that they moved to Asia Minor (Phrygia) and that his daughters lived long and served God to a very old age. We learn this tradition from Eusebius' quotes from both Polycrates and Papias (compare *Eccl. Hist.* 3:31:2–5).[163]

Philip the Evangelist, once known as one of "the Seven," now entertains the apostle Paul who was the reason that Philip fled from Jerusalem. Philip having had firsthand experience with the supernatural would have little difficulty accepting Paul who was once a persecutor of believers and now a believer who received a direct appeal from Jesus Christ.

Conclusion: Deacons developed during a time of quick expansion in the early Church. Persecution was rampant, and times were difficult in the community of God's people. In the early Church common property

---

[163] Robert James Utley, vol. Volume 3B, *Luke the Historian: The Book of Acts*, Study Guide Commentary Series (Marshall, TX: Bible Lessons International, 2003), 240.

served all and later ministries developed because of the need of widows and orphans. A complaint arose among a minority of believers out of which grew what is known today as Deacon Ministry. But this story is richer and far more important than a problem-solving exercise. It is the story of the Church growing. It is a story of God's hand weaving together circumstances, situations, and coincidences into many miracles like lights on a string. God is still shining the Gospel Light to all people.

The obligations of deacons involved in practical service, ministering to the physical needs of the church. Even today, deacons serve with the pastors or elders. They minister to the physical needs of the congregation and their communities. This is a valuable ministry, for deacons free the pastors and elders so they can give their full attention to the congregation's spiritual needs (Acts 6:2, 4).[164]

This is the primary function of deacons. Established deacons should not look at Stephen and Philip and learn nothing, but rather learn by their examples. The ministry of Stephen and Philip speaks well for them and for other deacons. Deacons should recognize that the boldness exhibited by Stephen and Philip can be theirs as well. Deacons should also recognize that the same Holy Spirit that motivated these two of the seven can move, inspire, and motivate them as well.

Congregations spend significant time and prayer in choosing deacons. Therefore, deacons should stand with boldness and aspire to be involved in ministry rejecting the administrative role and no longer be satisfied with the past status quo. Recapture the First Century deacon ministry and let Philip and Stephen be role models and examples to deacons everywhere.

Remember, when the deacon ministry began in the Church in Jerusalem this action of the local Church sparked massive numbers to come to Jesus. Remember in Acts 6, following the installation of the seven

---

[164] Max Anders, vol. 8, *Galatians-Colossians*, Holman New Testament Commentary (Nashville, TN: Broadman & Holman Publishers, 1999), 217.

deacons, revival broke out because of the deacon ministry concerning the ministry to the Widows.

Deacons are the most important public face of the local Church, more so than the Pastor, providing they are little "d" deacons. And that face needs to be loving, caring, evangelistic, and all the while pointing others to Jesus. Little "d" deacon ministry is crucial to the vibrant growth of the local Church. **This is the purpose and the end result of effective little "d" deacon ministry.**

www.ingramcontent.com/pod-product-compliance
Lightning Source LLC
Chambersburg PA
CBHW060511130626
46553CB00002B/460